# *How I Over*

# SOCIAL

# ANXIETY

## *(AND HOW YOU CAN TOO!)*

### AN INTROVERT'S *GUIDE* TO RECOVERING FROM SOCIAL ANXIETY, SELF-DOUBT AND LOW SELF-ESTEEM.

by

## TOBIAS J. ATKINS

http://www.socialanxietyacademy.com/

# Disclaimer

# CONTENTS

# FOREWORD

"**G**O APPROACH THAT GIRL and tell her she looks absolutely gorgeous" said the smooth looking Italian guy next to me with a mohawk and dark shades.

"Um, I…uh" my mouth immediately went dry and I tried to think of any reason not to go embarrass myself in the middle of Leicester Square in broad daylight.

"Come on, do it, before she walks away!" he insisted.

This was the first exercise on the first day of a Summer long program I joined - *at no small expense* - to build my confidence and competence with the opposite sex and I was considering dropping out before we even got started.

"Dude, last chance…"

So I walked over, heart pounding in my chest, and mustered up all the courage I could.

"Hi, excuse me," I stammered as I got her attention, "I just wanted to say that you look absolutely gorgeous today" as my face flushed and my knees almost buckled.

"Awwww, that's so sweet, thank you" and she smiled a genuinely appreciative smile.

"You're welcome. Well, um, have a great day" I said walking backwards a step or two before turning around and heading back to the coach who gave me a wink and a nod and said "Nice...now go tell her."

*This was going to be a long Summer.*

Fast forward 8 weeks and not only had I initiated conversations with well over 1,000 girls, some of which (fortunately) lasted more than 5 seconds, but I had completely transformed everything I thought I knew about social dynamics and human interaction. And in the years since I became a dating and confidence coach myself, working with hundreds of guys all around the world to help them overcome social anxiety and express themselves more confidently and congruently in all aspects of life.

I've worked with former U.S. Special Forces operatives who said they wouldn't think twice about running towards the sound of live ammunition, but couldn't muster the courage to give a girl a compliment. And I've worked with successful entrepreneurs and executives who manage teams of hundreds of people, but couldn't figure out why they were still single and lonely. It is a surprising phenomenon that something as simple as talking to a stranger can strike fear into the heart of the battle hardened and business savvy. But it turns out that the fear of rejection can be more powerful than the threat of clear and present danger.

Looking beyond the realm of dating and relationships, the reality is that a great many people experience social anxiety in some shape or form. Rationally it may not make any sense, and it's easy to resort to platitudes like *"If it doesn't work out, you'll be in the same place you are now."* But that doesn't speak to the emotional turmoil that accompanies the thought of being rejected, or worse derided, for speaking up and saying what is really on your mind.

Since you've picked up this book, there is a good chance that you have felt this way before and are looking for a solution to finally overcome the self-imposed pressures of being comfortable and at ease in social situations. If that is the case, then you're in the right place because in this book Tobias Atkins will share his story of struggling with, and ultimately overcoming a severe case of social anxiety, in addition to innumerable practical tips and strategies for how you can too.

If you're struggling with social anxiety, you may not think or believe that it is *actually* possible to overcome this condition. To manage or mitigate it perhaps, but not to *truly* move beyond the struggle and feel comfortably and at ease at work, at school, with friends and family, or even at a party. Well the good news is that you *can*, and by taking to heart the lessons Tobias shares, you will!

From doing a deep dive on your thoughts and beliefs, to analyzing your actions and exposure, Tobias provides a roadmap derived from his own personal journey from social paralysis to happiness and ease. Along the way he supplements his own experience with facts, science and actionable steps that you can take starting *today*.

That is not to say the journey will be easy or you can change deeply ingrained thought patterns and behaviors overnight. But it is to say that by taking incremental steps in a new direction, embracing new thought patterns and behaviors, and taking responsibility for creating the life you want and deserve, you *can* create a new reality for yourself. A reality where you look forward to going out, meeting new people and genuinely enjoying the company of others. That is the value of *How I Overcame Social Anxiety (And How You Can Too!)* and I hope this book serves you well today, tomorrow and all the days of your life.

To your social success,

**Jesse Krieger**
Founder of Lifestyle Entrepreneurs Press
Pisac, Peru

# ACKNOWLEDGMENTS

I've had many teachers along my journey, coming in many shapes and forms (anxiety being one of them). I would like to thank every one of them for providing me the lessons that have shaped me into the person I am today.

To all the people who have helped me in my life, there's no way I could ever fully repay you. However, I promise to do everything in my power to pay it forward.

I would like to dedicate this book to Derek & Jeff, the first people who ever made me truly believe I could overcome social anxiety. Thanks for believing in me when no-one else did. It means more to me than you could ever know.

# INTRODUCTION

## *What Is Social Anxiety (And How Do I Know if I Have It?)*

ACCORDING TO THE ADAA (Anxiety and Depression Association of America), anxiety disorders are the most common form of mental illness in the United States today, affecting approximately forty million adults ages eighteen and older. Social anxiety disorder (also known as social phobia) is estimated to affect 6.8 percent of the general population.[1]

Social anxiety has been described as:

> The fear of interaction with other people that brings on self-consciousness, nervousness, feelings of being negatively judged and evaluated, and, as a result, leads to avoidance. People with social anxiety feel they're constantly being negatively judged by other people and this leads to feelings of inadequacy, inferiority, embarrassment, humiliation, and depression.[2]

It's fairly normal for people to have times in their life when they feel a little shy or nervous, such as before giving a speech or going on a date. It becomes a problem when the fear of judgment and nervousness around people gets so intense it stops you from living a normal life and you begin to avoid everyday situations.

Signs and symptoms of social anxiety disorder can include:

- Fear of situations where you may be judged
- Fear of social gatherings and places where there may be many people
- Worrying about embarrassing yourself
- Intense fear of talking with strangers
- Fear that others are always watching and judging you
- Fear of physical anxiety symptoms such as blushing, sweating, trembling or having a shaky voice
- Avoiding doing things or speaking to people out of fear of embarrassment
- Avoiding situations where you might be the center of attention
- Having anxiety in anticipation of an upcoming activity or event
- Spending time after a social situation analyzing your performance and identifying flaws in your interactions
- Expecting the worst possible consequences from a negative social experience

Physical signs and symptoms can sometimes accompany social anxiety disorder and may include:

- Fast heartbeat
- Upset stomach or nausea
- Shortness of breath
- Sweating and blushing
- Shaky voice and stuttering
- Diarrhea
- Muscle tension

Common, everyday experiences that may be hard to endure when you have social anxiety disorder include, for example:

- Using a public restroom

- Interacting with strangers
- Talking in groups or to authority figures
- Eating in front of others
- Making eye contact
- Initiating conversations
- Dating
- Attending parties or social gatherings
- Attending work or school
- Job interviews
- Entering a room in which people are already seated
- Returning items to a store
- Standing up for yourself

These lead to avoidance behaviors such as:

- Not answering questions or giving your opinion
- Making excuses to leave early from situations that cause you anxiety
- Avoiding social situations whenever possible
- Pretending you're busy when someone invites you to an event
- Pretending you're okay with bad behavior to avoid conflict

*Note:* The above lists are not a substitute for a professional diagnosis.

## Why Get Help?

Social anxiety greatly affects people's overall quality of life. Not only does it hold people back from fulfilling relationships, it also affects physical health and financial success. Anxiety manifests itself in the human body as tightness, stress, and shortness of breath. Left unchecked, this leads to inflammation, a weakened immune system, and all kinds of stress-related illnesses.

Your career and financial success may also be suffering. People with social anxiety tend to avoid socializing in the workplace, asking for raises, talking to potential customers, and sharing their ideas. Some social anxiety sufferers have reported being thought of as a snobs or hard to get along with by their colleagues when, in reality, they're nice people who are just uncomfortable making small talk.

I think you can now see why it's so important we get this area handled. The good news is, it's a treatable condition, and many have had success in the past.

## *How Can I Help?*

If social anxiety is something you're dealing with, I want you to know there's nothing wrong with you. You're not weird or broken, you're not alone, and you don't have to suffer in silence anymore.

I have to point out that I'm not a qualified psychologist and the advice contained within this book is just my opinion. Although, having lived with anxiety disorders most of my life and recovered from them, I believe my opinion on this subject is worth considering. I've been professionally diagnosed with depression, social anxiety disorder, generalized anxiety disorder, and a form of OCD called obsessive, intrusive thinking. For a long period, I was on antidepressants and antianxiety medications. During the worst of it, I was on medical disability benefits due to my fear of job interviews.

The number of books published on anxiety disorders are into the hundreds, some being more effective than others. I know because I've read most of them. The majority of the books are written by qualified clinical psychologists, psychiatrists, and practitioners. Although they do offer some great advice that really works, I found many of the authors haven't lived through the conditions they're trying to help people with and they offer advice that they haven't actually tried themselves.

There is nothing necessarily wrong with that approach; however, on my journey I got the most help from people who have actually experienced social anxiety disorder themselves. It didn't seem to make much difference whether they were qualified or not, some were and others were not. I don't know whether this was because I trusted people who had been through social anxiety more, so I was more willing to listen to them, or because they could relate to what I was going through on an emotional level. Either way, this sentiment seems to hold true for many other people I have spoken with as well. Listening to someone with life experience who has actually been there seems to make the most difference.

Some of the most successful coaches in the world, including Tony Robbins, will tell you:

*"If you want to learn something, find someone who has already done what you want to achieve, study them, copy exactly what they did and you'll achieve the same results."*

For that reason, I've decided to share my story. If you're still struggling with social anxiety, I believe I can help you overcome it by sharing exactly what worked for me. My aim with this book is to share how I healed my anxiety disorders in a way that is easy to follow and understand, from the perspective of someone who's been in the trenches, suffered through it and come out the other side mentally healthy.

The focus of this book is social anxiety; however, the information and steps provided can also benefit in assisting with other forms of generalized anxiety and panic attacks as well as depression and perhaps even OCD. I'm someone who has lived with these debilitating conditions for twenty-seven years. Learning from someone who has been there will help you, as it did for me, when others shared their healing journey with me.

Change is possible. I'm not the first person to have overcome anxiety and I won't be the last either. If you get nothing else from this book other than those words, you're already halfway there because without believing you can overcome it, you'll find it hard.

I want to let you know there *is* light at the end of the tunnel, no matter how dark it seems right now. I truly hope this book helps you.

## *How to Get the Most out of This Book*

Congratulations. You've taken the most important step of the whole journey; you've sought help to improve your life. It's not weak to seek help. In fact, having the courage to seek help is one of the bravest things you can ever do. Be proud of yourself for that. The average person waits ten years before seeking help for social anxiety. Ten years is a very long time to be living with this condition.

To get the most from this book, you must read it with an open mind and be willing to look deep within yourself. I was able to change because I was willing to be really honest with myself, do some introspection, and figure out how my mind works. This isn't like Harry Potter—waving your wand, reciting an incantation and you're magically healed. This is a process that will require some effort and thinking on your part.

Treat the process of overcoming social anxiety like you would a work-out program or a diet; it takes a couple of months of hard work to start seeing solid results and it happens gradually. There's no magic pill or overnight cure. Anyone who tells you different is lying or hasn't been through the process themselves. That may not be what you want to hear right now but that is the truth.

Please don't give up on yourself if you put in a lot of effort but don't notice any change in the first week or two. Your unhelpful thought patterns probably have years of momentum behind them. Don't expect them to stop overnight. They will eventually go away, but it will take a bit of time and practice. Give yourself all the time you need without judgment.

You will need to read this book more than once. In fact, if you're struggling with any of the issues discussed and wish to overcome them, read it as many times as you need to until they are no longer an issue for you. Every single successful person I know says they read helpful books more than once. Highlight the parts that really stand out to you and reread them daily. The more you read them, the more the ideas discussed will sink in, and the easier it will be to change. There's a lot of information contained within this book, and it will be hard to remember it all in only one sitting.

If you're looking for any reason why this book won't work for you, you'll probably find it. When it comes to healing, we can only find that for which we search. You won't find healing by looking for all the reasons why you can't. Instead of fighting for your chains, choose to fight for your freedom.

This book was never meant to be a complete textbook on social anxiety and shouldn't be viewed it as such. If you're looking for that, there are plenty of other great books written by psychologists that go into much more detail about the science behind social anxiety. This book was written in a way that can be read many times over without having to sift through pages of unuseful information.

Many of the ideas discussed within this book are not my own and you may have already heard about them elsewhere. If so, accept my story as further confirmation that they actually work in the real world. Take some time to ponder the issues I struggled with and think about how they may apply to your current circumstances. While working with others, I've found that people with social anxiety have very similar thought patterns, even if the situations that provoke them may be different.

*Note: This book is not meant to be a substitute for a professional diagnosis or professional help. If you're suicidal, have severe agoraphobia, depression, or suffer from severe panic attacks in social situations, professional care is highly recommended.*

## *Born This Way? My Story*

I've had anxiety in one form or another ever since I was a young boy, and I've been in and out of psychologists' offices most of my adult life. If I added up all the money I've spent on doctor bills and medications, I probably could have bought a small island.

During my youth, I was always the shy one, easily upset by criticism, and I cried a lot. Added to this, I've always had fears that something was wrong with my health. These thoughts come and go but my favorite ones were: "I'm going to get a brain tumor" and "something is going to fall out of the sky onto my head and kill me." These thoughts showed up many times a day for many years.

I also suffered from frequent panic attacks that occurred at work, on the bus, or at home watching television. Anyone who has had such an episode knows the feeling; you honestly become convinced you're about to die. I remember my first one like it was yesterday. I was on a crowded bus coming home from work and it hit me. I couldn't escape from the situation and started hyperventilating in front of everyone on the bus. It was a very awkward bus ride home (for me anyway).

Social anxiety really came on strong for me as a teenager and young adult. My first really painful social experience came in my first year of high school. Everyone had to give a presentation in front of the class and I had been dreading it for weeks. I was one of the last ones to speak and by the time my turn came around I was already sweating and shaking with fear. As I stood in front of the class with my notes in hand, all I could see was everyone's eyes on me. That was the moment I froze. I tried to speak but the words wouldn't come out. I went totally blank.

As I was stuttering and stammering, trying to start my presentation, I heard some laughs coming from the back of the room. Eventually, the whole class erupted with laughter at this now bright red faced kid stuttering in front of them. That was about as much embarrassment as I could take and I burst out crying in front of my whole class. Then came the teasing.

As time went on, things got progressively worse. In public, I felt uncomfortable or awkward 90 percent of the time. I found it really difficult to relax and be myself around people, even with friends whom I had known for years and my own family. I was constantly monitoring my behavior, censoring my words and replaying awkward interactions over and over again in my head. Then I would beat myself up about how 'weak' and 'weird' I was. This was especially so in social gatherings. They were exhausting for me. No wonder I never wanted to go to any.

At parties or when meeting someone new, my voice would break up or I would be unable to speak, then I'd fake a phone call so I had an excuse to get out of there. I relied on binge drinking and hard drugs to help me to loosen up around people. Eventually, even that strategy stopped working and I ended up with serious side effects and a drug addiction that compromised my health.

I hated shopping malls. I remember walking through the supermarket to do my weekly shopping and feeling like I was naked, exposed and on display. I felt like everyone in the checkout line was staring at me, laughing and judging.

Like most people, I grew up believing the narrative we're sold by society. You were born confident or you weren't. You were good with people or you weren't. You either had it or you didn't, and I certainly didn't. Better luck next lifetime.

In social settings and at work, I would withdraw and fade into the background. I didn't like the attention being on me. Most people who knew me would say I was the "shy and silent type." This wasn't because I didn't have anything to say. I became silent because I was too scared to speak for fear of being judged for saying something stupid.

I began to avoid social situations like the plague. This isolation during my youth caused me to have underdeveloped social skills. I would do anything I could to avoid conflict because I couldn't handle anyone being angry at me; this meant agreeing with everything everyone said and never being able to say no to anyone. When I was a kid and even when I became a grown man in my twenties, I would sometimes cry if I got into an argument with someone. If someone said something hurtful to me, I would think about it and replay it over and over again in my mind for weeks or more, which was really exhausting.

*(This is very hard for me to share with the world. I haven't told many people outside of therapy about this, but it's a testament to how far I've come that I'm now comfortable enough to lay it all out there. A few years back there was no way I could have done this.)*

I kept silent about how I felt for many years, as I was afraid of being judged or called weird. When I did try to tell someone, I felt nobody really understood me and what I was going through. I was told things like "harden up" and "there's nothing to worry about." This made me feel even worse about myself. I felt very lonely inside, and I was craving intimacy and close relationships. At age twenty-four, I had never had a girlfriend. I was told by my psychiatrist that I had a chemical imbalance in my brain, and I had to take medication to rebalance it. This led me to believe that I was stuck with this thing called "anxiety" for life.

I took a variety of antidepressant medications on and off for many years. None of them worked very well for me personally, although I know others who have had success with them. Despite taking 5x the dose I started on, I still felt anxious and self-conscious. No matter where I went, I always felt there was something missing. Like there was an emptiness inside that could never be filled no matter how hard I tried with drugs, alcohol, and getting people to like me.

The lowest point in my life came while at university. When I was a kid, I had this picture in my mind about how awesome university would be. There would be parties, girls and loads of fun and adventure. University turned out nothing like the picture I had in my mind. I would go to my lectures, sit in the back row and come home without even speaking to a single person. I might as well have been there by myself!

I felt alone, helpless, and like there was no way out. I had completely lost hope of ever getting to experience the feeling of being in love or having a girlfriend. I couldn't even talk to my friends without getting nervous let alone a girl I didn't know. I contemplated suicide several times.

The catalyst for my change came after meeting a man who had recovered from social anxiety himself. For me, it wasn't enough just to be told how to do it by my psychologist. I needed to see evidence that social anxiety was beatable from someone who had actually been through it. Once I discovered that social anxiety was not a life sentence, I decided I would do anything it took to beat it too. This is how my journey of self-healing began. I spent every spare hour I had reading, listening to audiobooks, going to self-help programs, journaling, learning about myself and learning about anxiety. I sold all of my stuff and moved to the United States to seek out mentors.

I tried everything from CBT to psychoanalysis, medication to meditation, hypnosis to healthy eating, NLP (Neuro Linguistic Programming) to EFT (Emotional Freedom Techniques). I went to see Eastern healers, dating coaches, and life coaches. You name it; I tried it.

After spending well upwards of $35,000 on treatments during this period, I came to the conclusion that I was looking for one particular therapy as a 'cure all.' What I found was, most therapies helped but they were not enough on their own. Then I took only the ideas and techniques that worked for me from multiple therapies and mixed them together. What I'm about to share with you in this book has taken me many years of trial and error to figure out.

Today, many people I meet don't believe me when I tell them my history and the person I used to be (I take that as a huge compliment). I'm now totally comfortable talking to strangers. I love to go out to parties and bars and socialize, sometimes completely sober.

I realized my lifelong dream of becoming a club DJ. I've quit binge drinking and no longer take any form of drugs, prescription or otherwise. I've made so many new friends, and along the way, I developed the confidence to approach a really beautiful woman and start a conversation. She's now the love of my life. Yes, I finally experienced what it feels like to be in love! I wish you could see my face as I'm writing this because I have a big smile.

I've learned to like myself, be more assertive, and have let go of worrying about how others might see me. The most surprising revelation is I can now feel comfortable in my own skin without those judgmental voices in my head that used to derail everything I did. My hope is that I can help you begin to feel comfortable and happy being yourself too, and that is why I've written this book.

There's nothing different about me. What one person can do, so can another. I'm a regular guy who worked hard on myself. I know that if I can do it, you can too.

## Contributing Factors: There Was More than One

There are many other factors apart from genetics that can contribute to anxiety—lifestyle choices, limiting beliefs, negative thought patterns, past experiences, emotional scarring from past traumas, and avoidance or safety behaviors leading to poor social skills.

I've broken them down into three main areas to work on. These areas are:

1. Beliefs & Thoughts
2. Actions & Social Exposure
3. Lifestyle Choices & Diet

To get the best results, we must work on all three at the same time. If I had to pick the one most instrumental to my healing, it would be changing my thoughts and inner dialogue. But it wouldn't have been very effective if I had not been working on my lifestyle choices and avoidance behaviors at the same time.

Let me explain…

Getting out into the world and working on building your social confi-dence will not be as effective if you still have negative beliefs and self-talk going on (I'm ugly, boring, weird, no one likes me, etc.). If you try to treat the effects (behaviors) without fixing the real causes of social anxiety first (thoughts & beliefs), you'll likely burn out and want to quit after a short while.

Likewise, if you're highly stressed, not getting enough sleep, exercise, or sunlight and taking recreational drugs and alcohol, it's likely that this will be contributing to your anxiety too.

The rest of this book is a discussion of things I did differently in my life that helped me overcome not only social anxiety and shyness but all forms of my anxiety. All of the activities I've listed herein were very important in one way or another. If they didn't help, I wouldn't have listed them.

*Don't feel like you have to do all of these all at once. That would be too over-whelming. Do only what you can handle for now and take on more when you feel you're ready.*

# 1

# THOUGHTS & BELIEFS

*"The greatest discovery of all time is that a person can change his future by merely changing his attitude."* —Oprah Winfrey

*"Mind precedes all mental states. Mind is their chief; they are all mind-wrought. If with an impure mind a person speaks or acts, suffering follows him like the wheel that follows the foot of the ox. If, with a pure mind, a person speaks or acts, happiness follows him like his never-departing shadow."* —Dvedhavitakka Sutta

THOUGHT PRECEDES ALL. EVERY action, behavior, or emotion we've ever experienced in our life first originated with a thought. Before any kind of anxiety ever manifested in our physical body, a thought came before it. Thus, we must examine our thoughts first if we want to fix the real causes of our anxiety. This is the most important chapter in the book, and that's why it's first.

## *The Two Prison Fences*

I want to start off by sharing with you the quote that completely changed the course of my life:

*"Social anxiety and shyness is not a life sentence."*

That's right, you can get over social anxiety. I know what some of you may be thinking right now because I was telling myself the same thing.

*"Anyone who got over social anxiety must not have had it as bad as me. I have it BAD, really bad. There's no way I'll ever get over my social anxiety. I was born this way, it's genetic, and there's nothing I can do..."*

This is what I would tell myself if I ever heard about someone who recovered from social anxiety. Hidden in that quote are two beliefs that are responsible for keeping more people stuck for life than all the others combined. Those beliefs are...

1. *"I was born this way and there's nothing I can do to change it."*
2. *"Change is easy for others but not for me because my situation is different and much worse."*

These two limiting beliefs act like the two fences in a prison, trapping anyone who believes them from ever escaping their self-imposed prison of fear.

# Fence #1

"I was born this way" manages to keep most people trapped for their whole lives without even reaching the second fence. Most of us grow up believing either you have social confidence or you don't. We tell ourselves things like "I was born shy; it runs in my family." This kind of "have it or you don't" thinking is further reinforced when we hear phrases such as "A tiger never changes it stripes" and "You can't teach an old dog new tricks."

Holding beliefs like this is very detrimental for your growth and leads to feelings of helplessness. If you believe something is out of your control, you don't even bother trying to change it. You've struck out before you even get up to bat. Or you may have already tried to overcome your social anxiety and shyness in the past and it didn't work out, further confirming your belief that something is inherently wrong with you, you're beyond help, or you have a genetic fault in your brain.

It's important to keep in mind that many people don't find success the first few times they try something new. It's been said by *Business Insider* that many successful business owners fail once or more before they succeed.[3] I believe it's the same with overcoming social anxiety. It took me years of trial and error to get where I am today. It's especially hard if you don't have the right information and tools. Don't worry though, after reading this book you will have everything you need to know in order to succeed.

Genetics does play a part in social anxiety but it has been scientifically proven that genetic expression can be changed by thoughts, environment, emotions, and beliefs. Genetics certainly shouldn't be used as an excuse to give up before you've even tried or because you may have tried once before and it didn't work out.[4]

I want you to know you don't have to live with social anxiety forever. Even if you think you were born this way, you can get over feeling anxious around people. You can even get to a stage where you're… gasp… excited to meet new people. I know all of this firsthand because it happened for me.

## Fence #2

If people ever get a hint of getting past the first fence, such as seeing someone else recover from social anxiety, the next belief is right there to keep them stuck.

*"Change is easy for others but not for me because my situation is different and much worse."*

I don't want to come across as condescending, but almost every person I've ever met with social anxiety has this belief, including me for many years. The law of averages alone means this belief can't be true for everyone. Wouldn't you agree it's fair to assume that in a world of seven billion people, there have been at least a few people with anxiety as bad as yours who recovered from it? You need to become open to the possibility that it may be your thoughts, beliefs and lifestyle choices that are contributing to your social anxiety, not factors out of your control.

In no way, shape, or form am I downplaying your situation or saying you don't have it bad. What I am suggesting is that you have the power to heal yourself and change your life, no matter where you currently are. What's the alternative? Go on believing you're beyond help and live out your days as they are now without any hope of change?

I'll expand on this point later in the book, but this was a really important part of my healing. I had to get past blaming circumstances out of my control and look inward. Then I began to see all the things I was doing that were contributing to my anxiety, nervousness around others, and poor self-esteem. Before that, I wasn't even aware I was doing any of these things; they just fell under the category of "that's just the way I am. I was born this way and I'm beyond help."

Does it make you excited to know that change is possible for you? If you already believe it, great! You're already 50 percent there. However, in my experience, most people get stuck on those two beliefs, as I was.

## *Wanting Someone Else to Fix You*

Did you know not even the greatest doctor in the world can heal you? Sure, he can tell you what is wrong with you and what needs to be changed. He can even operate on you, but he can't fix you or heal you.

*Only you can heal you.*

Always looking for someone else to fix you takes your own healing power away. For as long as you believe someone else needs to fix you, you will remain stuck. You're the only one in control of your life. The sum of all your choices got you to this point, and only you can get out of it. Sure, there are great teachers who can help you and show you the way, but they can't do it for you. They can only lead you to the door; you must walk through it yourself by stepping into your power and putting what you've learned into practice.

# *Acceptance without Judgment: I Stopped Beating Myself Up*

*"If you find yourself in a hole, stop digging."* —Will Rogers

Are you someone who constantly beats yourself up for having social anxiety? If so, I want to share with you something that may help you go a little easier on yourself. Social anxiety is your brain's way of keeping you safe. It's not out to get you and there is nothing inherently wrong with you. Let me explain...

As we grow up, we encounter plenty of painful social experiences. Our childhood crush tells us she would rather die than date us. Our friends tell us we are ugly and fat. We get nervous while giving a presentation and the whole class laughs at us for messing it up.

Your personality may have already been on the sensitive side, but add in a few of these painful social experiences, (mixed with other factors like putting too much importance on the opinions and judgments of others), and your brain learns to associate social situations with the potential for massive pain.

Now, when you get into a social situation, your brain triggers the fight, flight or freeze response, releasing stress hormones into your body that cause you to tense up, sweat and blush etc. Social anxiety is your brain's way of telling you to get the hell out of what it perceives to be a dangerous situation as soon as possible. Even though this behavior is no longer serving you, it's important to realize your brain is only trying to keep you safe and protected. There's nothing inherently wrong with you and you're not 'weak' or 'broken'. You just have some unhelpful associations in your brain right now.

The first thing I had to do to get over my social anxiety was to accept and make peace with who I was and where I was. I had to learn to use self-compassion and accept myself even with social anxiety and all my flaws. Let me tell you, it definitely wasn't easy to accept myself with this condition.

Prior to this, I was constantly fighting with myself, feeling inferior to everyone because I was so anxious, feeling like a failure and a lesser person, wondering why it happened to me. Not only was I feeling anxious, but I was also getting angry and putting myself down for feeling anxious; it was a double whammy of negative emotions. I understood that if I were ever going to get over this condition, I needed to quit beating myself up for having it.

The first thing I did was repeat to myself, "This is where I currently am and as much as I don't like it, I know this social anxiety doesn't say anything about my worth as a person, so I guess I'm okay even with social anxiety."

I use that term a lot now with myself. It's okay to not be perfect, it's okay to sometimes say the wrong thing and have an awkward conversation, it's okay that I sometimes feel shy and nervous around people. Instead of scolding myself for my flaws and all the times I messed up,

I let go of the judgment. Boy does it feel nice to let go of judging yourself all the time. It was as if a weight had been lifted off my shoulders.

Your anxiety or self-consciousness in any given situation will eventually subside; however, the feelings of shame, self-rejection, and self-hate will stay around much longer. Those cause more damage than the actual anxiety itself. The next time you encounter a situation that causes you anxiety. Instead of thinking, *Oh no, this shouldn't be happening! This is bad! Why am I so weak?* and trying to fight it and hold it back, try letting it happen and accept that it's okay you're currently feeling anxious. It's your brain's way of trying to keep you safe. Practice self-compassion and begin treating yourself like you would a close friend who was going through what you're currently going through.

Letting go and letting it happen instead of judging and trying to fight it feels a little counterintuitive, but it will prevent you from feeling even worse while it's happening. Anyway, you've probably already discovered you can't use force to stop anxiety from happening even if you wanted to, and getting angry at yourself about it only makes things far worse.

The first step to healing is accepting where you currently are. Accepting your situation doesn't mean you have to be happy about it or even like it. It means facing the fact that it's here and, at this point, it is happening. It's saying to yourself, *"For whatever reason, right now, I have these things I don't like about myself, but I chose to love myself anyway, even with all my flaws."*

This is such a crucial point and I want you to understand just how important practicing self-acceptance and self-compassion is. Just because you feel anxious around people doesn't make you a weak or inferior person. Your anxiety is not *you*. You simply have some behaviors that aren't serving you right now; it doesn't say anything at all about your worth as a person.

It was only after accepting where I was and letting go of fighting it that I could begin to change. Don't get me wrong, there were days when those frustrated "what's wrong with me and why is this happening to me?" thoughts would come up. I just chose to ignore them as much as I could and stopped rejecting myself over my anxiety. I understood it was my brain's way of trying to keep me safe and that helped me to feel better about my situation.

## Key Points

1. Go easy on yourself! No amount of beating yourself up about your weaknesses will ever make them better, only worse. Let your new mantra be "It's okay."
2. Be more kind to yourself. You need to accept where you currently are without judgment to move forward.

# *You Should Stop Shoulding Yourself*

One way lack of self-acceptance can show up is when we talk in should statements.

*"I should be funnier."*
*"I should be mentally stronger."*
*"I shouldn't feel this nervous around people."*
*"This anxiety shouldn't be happening to me."*

Every time your mind throws you a "should," don't pay attention to what comes after. Shoulds are the exact opposite of self-acceptance. Self-acceptance says, "You are where you are and that's ok." Shoulds say, "Feel guilty and ashamed about who you are and this condition." Shoulds bring on feelings of guilt, embarrassment and shame. They never help with anxiety and only ever serve to make you feel worse about yourself. You *should* stop shoulding yourself as soon as possible.

# *I Focused More on the Solution (and Less on the Problem)*

Talking about and justifying all the reasons for my social anxiety was not the solution for me. Doing something to change it was. Have you ever noticed that focusing on your flaws, weaknesses, and past struggles never makes you feel better? No, it only ever makes you feel worse. So, why do we continue to do it? It's probably because we've formed a habit of doing it, a habit that can be broken now we're aware it's not helping us.

What helped me break this habit was to focus less on the problem and more on the solution. Instead of continually asking myself, "What's wrong with me, why am I always so shy and nervous around people?" (the problem). I began to focus on what it would look like and feel like to be the person I desired to be (the solution).

I visualized and felt in my body how it would feel to have a conversation that didn't feel awkward. I saw myself confidently talking in a group of people and making them laugh. It felt good to be this super confident person, so I kept doing it as much as I could. Then I chose to focus less on all the things I wanted to change about myself because that didn't make me feel good. Listen to your emotions and ask yourself constantly:

*"Is what I'm thinking about myself right now making me feel good?"*

If so, keep doing it; if not, change the subject. You have the power to choose what you think about. Why not choose a thought that makes you feel good instead of bad? Now you're probably saying:

*"If only it were that easy, of course I would choose a helpful thought if I could, but I can't help what I think about. It just happens."*

23

Trust me, with some time and practice you'll be able to better control your thoughts. For now, just become aware as much as you can throughout the day of when you're feeling negative emotions, and do your best not to go there anymore.

As I spent more time focused on the person I desired to be, I allowed that person to show himself because I wasn't so focused on the present and my current flaws. By focusing only on what's wrong, you keep yourself stuck and unable to grow into anyone new. Plus it just doesn't feel good; so why continue to do it?

*Later in the book, I'm going to talk more about the life-changing power of positive visualization and explain exactly how to do it to get the best results.*

## Key Points

1.  Form a picture in your mind of your perfect self. Think about exactly who you desire to be.
2.  Focus only on the person you desire to be and forget your current flaws as much as you can.

# *I Took My Power Back (The Victim Mentality)*

My whole life I had been trying to please and accommodate everyone at the expense of my own happiness. I would bend over backward for total strangers because I didn't want to feel the awkwardness of disapproval or having to say no to someone (and the guilt that would stir up in me).

I believed that everyone should be happy all the time, and if they weren't, it was my job to fix it. I went out of my way for everyone to make sure they liked me. Everyone had to like me for me to feel good about myself. If someone didn't like me, I would worry and fret about it and have to make it right with that person as soon as possible, even if they were in the wrong. I had totally given other people the power to control how I felt, so it shouldn't come as a surprise I felt like crap most of the time.

I was a total yes man. Sometimes I would say yes before the person had even finished asking me the favor, even if I didn't want to do it. I used to put everyone's needs above my own, and the way I would justify it was by telling myself I was being a good person and *"good people always put others first."* What I was really doing, however, was rejecting myself and my needs, and my self-esteem suffered greatly because of it. If this is something that you do, I would guess it's contributing to your symptoms too.

I grew up in a house with strict parents who used to smack me whenever I answered back or didn't do what they wanted. Like a lot of kids who grow up in this situation, I soon learned not to talk back and to do whatever they told me. No wonder I grew up letting people walk all over me. It was my subconscious mind's way of protecting me:

*"Be submissive and quiet; please people and you'll be safe."*

That belief followed me right into adulthood. Here's a list of things that I grew up listening to over and over again. Maybe some of these will sound familiar to you:

*"Do as you're told."*
*"Don't talk back."*
*"Ssshh, let the adults speak."*
*"Don't argue."*
*"Don't fight."*

*"Always respect your elders."*
*"Always serve yourself last."*
*"Always share with others; don't be selfish."*

Here are some of the things I was told by my friends, teachers, and people in the community while I was growing up.

*"You're ugly."* (*I heard that one a lot.*)
*"You're fat."*
*"You'll never amount to anything."*
*"You look like you're twelve years old."* (*When I was eighteen.*)
*"You're a bad kid."*
*"You were born into sin/you're a sinner."*
*"No woman would want to go out with you."*
*"Guys like you don't date women like that."*
*"Tobi is the awkward one of the group."*

These comments hurt me immensely and caused me deep trauma. I consider myself a nice and fairly nonjudgmental person, so I couldn't understand why everyone was so mean to me when I was young. Well, to be honest, not everyone was mean to me, but my belief was:

*"People are judgmental, hurtful, and unkind."*

Because I believed that, my brain only looked for the bad in people and I paid little attention to all the good things that happened to me in my life. I began to resent other people and blame them for my circumstances. This kind of thinking turned me into a victim.

I see a common pattern on the anxiety forums. Some people are so attached to their history of hurt that it's become their identity. They're still upset over what someone did to them in the past or how bad their circumstances were and they can't seem to let it go. They talk about it with their psychologists, and they post about it on the forums, looking for people to sympathize and agree with them about how bad they have it.

I'm not one to judge; I did this very thing for years. I had so many situations growing up in which I was judged, ridiculed, rejected, told I was worthless by people close to me, and abused physically and mentally. I couldn't wait to tell anyone who was willing to listen how bad I had it, especially my psychologist. I was looking for sympathy and I got it, but no matter how much I got, other people's sympathy didn't heal me.

Here's the thing about our stories. The majority of us grew up with dysfunctional families or around dysfunctional, negative people. Everyone has their stories about how other people hurt them and why they are the way they are.

## Here Are Some Examples...

"My parents beat me and abandoned me; that's why I have low self-esteem now."

"My parents were strict and smacked me when I answered back; that's why I let people walk all over me today."

"My friends told me I'm ugly and fat; that's why I feel nervous around people now."

"My whole life, people have been telling me I'm inferior and I'll never amount to anything; that's why I don't feel good about myself and sabotage my success."

"My whole life, people have been treating me like dirt; that's why I continue to treat myself like dirt."

"My boyfriend/girlfriend cheated on me and now I can't trust anyone."

"I was dealt an unlucky hand. My anxiety is genetic; it runs in the family, and there's nothing I can do about it."

Everyone believes their situation is unique and that healing may be easy for other people but not for them. The truth is, the more we think we're different, the more we are the same. We must begin to realize that our stories about how other people hurt us aren't helping us heal and grow; they're keeping us stuck in a "poor me" victim mentality.

For twenty-seven years, I blamed everybody but myself for the state of my life: my parents, my friends, my community. It was never me but always someone else's fault. I was never studying my actions or looking inward. I was always looking outward for someone to blame, and, as a result, my life sucked. Once I began taking full responsibility for my own happiness, thoughts, and behaviors, I started seeing change.

*Are you more interested in getting where you want to go or defending where you are? Would you rather feel sorry for yourself and blame other people or heal yourself and be happy?*

This isn't to say that people haven't been telling you that you're worthless, ugly, weird, etc. for years, probably since you were a young impressionable child. But it's always our choice what we believe. People can tell us hurtful things, but they can't make us believe it without our consent.

You decide who and what you are, not someone else. The moment we realize this is the moment we take the power back in our lives. Then we can begin to say:

"THIS STOPS TODAY! I'm no longer willing to believe what I've been told about myself all my life. I'm no longer going to treat myself like an inferior, worthless person because of what someone else said or did to me in the past."

"I'm no longer going to give other people the power to make me feel ugly, stupid, inferior, uncool, worthless or embarrassed because no one can make me feel anything without my permission. I'm not a victim; I'm the one in control of my thoughts and how I feel, and from this day forward I choose to like myself."

You can only begin to take your power back in your life when you stop playing the role of the helpless victim. Before you get defensive, I'm not saying you should ever blame yourself for what others said and did to you, but you must understand that your beliefs and actions are always in *your* control—no one else's.

You are not responsible for the treatment you received as a child or for the negative things other people told you when you were too young to know any better. However, you *are* responsible for fixing it now as an adult. No one else is going to do it for you because no one else can do it for you.

Your past stories of hurt did happen and people probably did some horrible things to you. No one is ever going to deny that. I'm not saying what happened to you in your past wasn't terrible, but now you have a choice about where you're going to go from here.

Are you going to let your past continue to ruin today for you? Are you going to continue treating yourself like dirt just because everyone else has in the past? Are you going to keep holding onto your stories and excuses that are keeping you trapped and disempowered? You know, the stories about how you're a failure at everything, you're worthless and not capable of much.

Or are you today, in this moment, going to turn a new page and choose a more empowering story for yourself? A story of victory, not failure.

It's always your choice what story you choose to tell yourself.

Let the past go. Forgive anyone who wronged you in the past and move on. Your parents, family, caregivers, and friends were just doing what they knew how to do with their limited awareness. People can't give you something they don't have. Also, forgive yourself for anything you've done in the past that you're not proud of and all the times you messed up.

The past is over and it can't be changed no matter how badly you feel about it. No amount of hate, guilt, or shame will ever change the past. What hate, guilt, and shame will do, however, is ruin today for you. Living in the past is the best way to keep getting the exact same results in the future.

Yesterday is over, today is a new day, and today you can choose to be anyone you want to be. No matter how much your past sucked, let it go. You may look back one day and see it becomes your greatest source of strength and greatest learning lesson.

*As a side note, EFT was a crucial part in helping me let go of some my past traumas. I will go into more detail about EFT later in the book.*

# Key Points

1.  It's time to let go of your past disempowering stories and move forward. Stop talking about them and looking for sympathizers. It's keeping you stuck in a "poor me" victim mentality.
2.  Be no longer willing to give other people the power to make you feel worthless, inferior, nervous, or embarrassed. You are in control of your life, no one can make you believe anything without your permission.

# "Hi I'm Tobi and I Aim to Please" (People Pleasing)

As I was saying, I had given everyone else the power to control my emotions. If they liked me, I felt good; if not, I felt terrible and would obsess about it for days. I walked through the world constantly fearing judgment and the pain it would cause me. This made me close off, clam up, and be afraid to show the real me.

Because of my fear of other people's disapproval, I ended up trying to be everything to everyone. I was one of those fake people who agrees with everything everyone says. I would change my preferences and likes, depending on who I was talking to. If it was someone who liked boxing, I liked boxing. If it was someone who hated boxing, I hated boxing. I would agree to do things I didn't want to do to in order to gain acceptance, then either cancel via text last minute or do it begrudgingly and resent them for asking me.

I had no idea what my values were, who I was, and what I stood for. So I would easily get manipulated, led astray, and knocked off course like a boat out at sea without a rudder. My identity and values became lost in all the trying to fit in and getting others to like me...

## An Old Man, His Son, and a Donkey Walk into a Bar...

One of my favorite Aesop's fables goes like this. A man and his son were once walking with their donkey to market. As they were walking, they passed an old woman who said, "You fools, what is a donkey for but to ride upon?" So the man put the boy on the donkey and they went on their way.

As they walked, they soon passed a group of men, one of whom said, "See that lazy youngster, what kind of son lets his father walk while he rides?" So the boy, feeling guilty, got off the donkey and let the father on. But they hadn't gone far when they passed two young women, one of whom said to the other, "Shame on that lazy father to let his poor little son walk while he rides."

Well, by this stage, the man and boy didn't know what to do. At last, they decided to both hop up on the donkey and continue on their way. Before long, they could see the town, and as they approached, the passers-by began to jeer and point at them. The man stopped and asked what they were scoffing at. The men said, "You should be ashamed of yourselves for overloading that poor donkey with you and your fat son."

The man and boy, both feeling guilty, got off and tried to think of what to do. They thought and they thought, till at last they cut down a pole, tied the donkey's feet to it, and both started carrying the donkey. They went along amid the laughter of all who met them till they came to a bridge. The donkey, getting one of his feet loose, kicked out and caused the boy to drop his end of the pole.

In the struggle, the donkey fell over the bridge and, since his forefeet were tied together, drowned. "That will teach you for being so stupid. Donkeys are meant to be ridden, not carried," said an old man who had followed them.

The moral: *You can't please everyone. No matter what you do, there will be some who find fault in it.*

This parable sums up how silly it is to try to please everybody and worry about what they think of you. You may think this is only a fable, but real life works in much the same way. No matter what you do and how much you try, there will always be those who judge and find fault with what you're doing.

# You Do You & I'll Do Me (Some People Will Always Judge)

*"The greatest prison people live in is the fear of what other people think."*—David Icke

People have opinions about everything. Most people form opinions about things they know nothing about, including you. I find it insane just how many people comment on issues they know nothing about but act like they're an authority on the subject. That just reconfirms how little attention we should pay to other people's opinions and comments. Most of it is just hot air based on nothing. I spent my whole life running from the fear of other people's disapproval. Not only was it exhausting, but I realized no matter what I did, I couldn't escape it anyway.

I'm going to give it to you straight; no matter what you do, there will be a few people out there who are just not going to like you. Most people you meet will either like you or be indifferent. However, usually about 5 to 10 percent of people won't like or agree with you and some will be *very* vocal about it. I know that no matter what I do and how much I try to be perfect and please others, there are people out there who aren't going to like me. And what I've come to realize is—that's fine; not everyone has to like me.

I know that in writing this book and trying my best to help people by sharing my story with the world, some people will make some negative comments about me and the book. That's just the way it is. Today, I don't let that fear stop me from living my life and doing what I think is right, and you shouldn't let it stop you from living your life either. I spent twenty-seven years letting that fear stop me; I know exactly where that road leads, and it's not a place I want to live anymore.

*"There is only one way to avoid criticism, do nothing, say nothing, and be nothing."* —Aristotle

# I Stopped Accepting Other People's Opinions as Facts

In my life I've been called ugly, fat, dumb, loser, shy, selfish, not good enough, out of her league, weird, boring and egotistical (that's just to name a few). Instead of seeing those comments for what they were— just some random person's untrue opinion—I began to believe what other people told me about myself and took it onboard as my identity.

Like we discussed, when most people give their opinion about something, they talk as if it's a scientifically proven fact. For example, people tend to say things such as:

"This music is crap."

"She's ugly."

"He's a loser."

"She's not very smart."

**However, what they're really saying is:**

"I THINK this music is crap."

"I THINK she's ugly."

"I THINK he's a loser."

"I THINK she's not very smart."

*Big difference.*

This is a very important concept to grasp. For years and years, I allowed myself to be conned by people who talked as if their opinion was a proven fact. It's vital to be able to differentiate opinion from fact so you don't get swept up in people's opinions about you and take them onboard as truth. You need to train yourself to become consciously aware that when someone is saying something negative about you, it's not the truth; it's simply an opinion.

There will be some people out there who will call you "uncool" while others will call you "too cool." There may be people out there who call you a "nerd" while others call you "dumb." Some people are going to think you're attractive and others won't.

So who is right? With all these contradictory opinions about you, they can't all be fact. When someone has a negative opinion about you, it isn't right or wrong; it's just their opinion, and people's opinions are subjective, not fact. Regardless of how other people view you, you're the same person. It's others' perception of you that differs, and that's never in your control. Worrying about what others think of you is a game you can never win. Throw your hands up in the air and say, *"I quit!"*

Sure, it's not nice when someone says something bad about you, and, even though we know it's only an opinion and it's going to happen from time to time, it still hurts. The key is to not take it onboard as truth and not allow it to make you feel bad about yourself. Imagine your favorite type of music. You know there are people in the world who can't stand that type of music, and they will be very quick to let you know. You're not going to stop listening to it just because there are some who don't like it, right? So why then should it be any different when it comes to how you feel about yourself? Why would you reject yourself just because there are some who don't like you?

To paraphrase the late Wayne Dyer:

*Every time you find yourself anxious, upset, depressed or embarrassed over what someone thinks of you or has said about you, what you're really saying in that moment is, what you think of me is more important than how I feel about myself.*[5]

If this is something you can relate to, I want you to ask yourself...

*Why should you continue to fear judgment from other people when you know it's not fact?*

*Why should you continue to let other people's opinions make you feel badly about yourself?*

*Why are you giving other people the power to control how you feel?*

Whenever you give other people the power to control how you feel, you have just put them in charge of you. This strategy never ends well. Again, no judgment and no beating yourself up. Just be curious as to why you feel what others think of you should be placed above how YOU feel. If you keep asking yourself these types of questions whenever you encounter criticism or the fear of judgment, over time, you'll begin to feel less and less concerned about it.

What other people think of you doesn't matter, the only thing that matters is that you like and accept yourself. If you don't currently feel good about yourself, I'm going to show you several ways you can change that soon.

You may be thinking at this point:

*"To stop caring so much what others think about me is much easier said than done. It's not like I want to care; I just can't help it."*

I know. I understand. I was exactly the same. But it is *possible* to care less what others think. It's not a realistic (or even advisable) goal to 100 percent stop caring what others think, but you can certainly get to a point where others' opinions become background noise instead of a crippling roadblock.

Just keep reminding yourself: *What other people think of me is 100 percent out of my control, and some people will judge me no matter what I do. So in knowing that, I might as well be myself and let the chips fall where they may.*

The more you reread this chapter and let it really sink in, the more detached you'll become from the opinions of others. When you become detached from the opinions of others, the less you'll fear judgment in social situations and this will make it easier to relax.

# Key Points

1. There are seven billion individuals sharing this planet, all with different likes and opinions. Some people will like you and some won't. That's not important. What's important is that you like yourself.
2. What other people think of you is 100 percent out of your control, so it makes no sense to waste energy trying to control something that is out of your control.

3. When you're comfortable with who you are and become detached from the opinions of others, you'll lower your social anxiety.

# *Are You a People Pleaser and Approval Seeker?*

Are you still unsure whether you may have the traits of a people pleaser or an approval seeker? Here are some telltale signs. (I should know because I did almost all of these things on a regular basis.)

1. You have trouble saying no to people. You agree to things when you really want to say no.
2. You're always apologizing for everything you do, even when it's not your fault. For example, someone steps on your feet, and YOU apologize to them.
3. You're passive aggressive and avoid confrontation at all costs. You're nice when you don't really feel that way.
4. You feel like everyone must be happy all the time, and if someone is upset, it's your job to make them feel better.
5. When someone does the wrong thing by you, you let it slide because you don't want to hurt anyone's feelings and create a scene. Instead, you choose to suffer in silence and you justify it by telling yourself you're a nice person who is above arguing.
6. You have trouble falling asleep at night worrying if someone doesn't like you.
7. You must be liked by everyone all the time. If someone doesn't like you, it's a big deal.
8. You believe you should always put others first, and you feel guilty for putting your needs first.
9. You're afraid of being criticized, especially being told you're selfish.

10. You overpromise and agree to do things that aren't right by you.
11. You only feel good if others like you and say nice things about you. If they don't, you feel worthless and terrible.
12. You feel like you must always be nice to people, no matter what.

# Here Are Some Approval-Seeking Behaviors You May Be Doing.

1. Always agreeing with everyone, even when you don't really agree with what they said.
2. Changing your opinion to fit who you're talking to, or if someone disagrees with you.
3. Saying what you think people want to hear, not what you actually think or feel.
4. Always going along with what others want to do and not wanting to rock the boat.
5. Never complaining about bad service or returning a poor product to avoid conflict.
6. Always asking someone else's approval before you do anything such as, "Do you mind if I ask you a question? Or, "Do you mind if I run to the bathroom."
7. Giving into peer pressure and being easily persuaded to do things you don't want to do.
8. Being afraid to say or do the wrong thing, so you do and say nothing and fade into the background.
9. Lying that you've heard of a certain band, movie, etc. when you actually haven't because you don't want to seem uncool.

Those are some of the main traits of people pleasers and approval seekers. Can you identify with some of those? Remember, NO JUDGMENT! This list isn't designed to make you feel bad about yourself, only to help you realize there's something that needs to change. I hope you're able to see now how these traits might be contributing to your social anxiety and low self-esteem and how when you stop doing them, you'll like yourself much more.

*"I've decided to stop saying yes to people and situations that don't support my well-being. Instead, I will say yes to my happiness, and yes to my growth, and yes to all the people and things that inspire me to be authentic and whole, while at the same time accepting me just as I am. My yes, from here on out, is my pledge to live honestly, my commitment to love myself fiercely, and my cry to create my best life possible. Yes."* —Scott Stabile

# Who Am I? (Get Clear on Exactly Who You Are)

*"If I want to be free, I've got to be me. Not the me others think I should be. Not the me my wife thinks I should be. If I want to be free, I've got to be me. So I better find out exactly who the real me is."* —Bill Gove

I began to get over my people-pleasing and approval-seeking habits when I took some time to think about what my values are. Who I am, what I like and don't like, what I stand for, and what I will and won't accept.

With the help of some books, mentors, and real friends, I realized that it's okay to be myself and to speak my mind. I learned it's okay to disagree with people and tell people no. I accepted that no matter what I did, some people wouldn't agree with it, and the sun will still rise tomorrow even if people didn't like me or agree with me.

Take some time to really think about who you are, what you like, what your values are, and what you stand for. Then be proud of those things; don't hide them away and be ashamed of them. You like what you like, you want what you want, and you feel how you feel. Never be afraid to be exactly who you are, and never let anyone try to convince you it's wrong. Practice being honest and authentic with yourself and others. The world doesn't need seven billion carbon copy replicas who all like the same things and agree with one another; the differences in people are what makes life fun and why we have so much variety to choose from.

The reality is, people don't respect someone who doesn't respect him or herself. Make it a priority to be yourself, respect yourself, and voice your opinions. Sure, it's nice when other people like you; however, if you NEED other people to like you in order to feel good about yourself, you're handing the key to your happiness over to someone else and setting yourself up for a life of pain.

*If you can identify with any of the traits mentioned so far in the book and would like more help in resolving them once and for all, I have created a five-hour self-esteem building course on my website. www.socialanxietyacademy.com.

# *Are You an Honest Person?*

I want to ask you a question: *Do you think you're an honest person?*

If you do, then wouldn't you agree that saying yes when you want to say no is not being honest? How about agreeing when you don't really agree? Is that being honest? What about pretending to be interested in something that you're really not into in order to get people to like you? Every time you pretend to be someone you're not, what you're really saying is, "I don't feel I'm good enough as I am, so I need to act like someone different for you to like me and approve of me." Ugh, there's that nasty self-rejection again.

When I went through this process, I noticed a contradiction. I thought of myself as honest, but when I asked myself these questions, I found I wasn't being honest with myself or others. This process helped me to see that saying how I truly felt and being honest was the best thing to do. It allowed me to feel more comfortable disagreeing with people and voicing my opinion.

It doesn't mean you always have to give unsolicited negative opinions or tell someone about all their flaws, but when it comes to how people are making you feel and voicing your preferences, you should always try to be honest with them and yourself. Honesty is the best policy, and that means speaking up.

You can't help but respect someone who's honest. These days, an honest and authentic person is becoming harder to find. However, most people would tell you it's one of the most appreciated traits you can have in a friend. Most people want someone who isn't afraid to tell them the truth and give an honest opinion as long as it comes from a constructive place. I always appreciate honesty and authenticity in my life, even when I don't like the answer.

# Why Do I Care So Much What Others Think of Me?

Throughout this process of change, it's so important to be easy on yourself and let go of judging yourself negatively. We were brought up to care what others think of us. As children, our well-being and success in life depended on the approval of others. If we didn't have our parents' approval, we learned quickly there would be pain and suffering for us. If we didn't have our teachers' approval, there would be pain and suffering too.

We learned from a young age that we get more rewards and positive feedback when we offer behavior that pleases our providers. So being a dependent and needing them for our survival, it makes sense that we try we please them as much as we can.

As adults, we still need people to survive; we need food, clothes, shelter, and medical help. We want friends and companions who care about us. We want to attract a mate and find love. We want to look good in front of the boss, etc. Caring what other people think of us can be helpful for our lives; otherwise, we would all be slobs and never shave, take showers or dress well.

A little bit of self-consciousness helps to remind us to be aware of how our actions are affecting those around us. We don't want to be the loud, obnoxious talker in the movie theater or the person who never lets anyone else talk in a conversation. So, there's nothing fundamentally wrong with caring what others think; it's just when it gets out of hand and stops us from living a normal healthy life that we need to keep it in check.

## Further Reading

If this is something you struggle with, I recommend reading *Pulling Your Own Strings* by Wayne W. Dyer. This book was monumental in helping me stop being a people pleaser and approval seeker. I've probably read it twenty times or more.

# *Are You a Mind Reader?*

Another thing to remember is how little people actually do even judge. People have their own problems to worry about; they're not worrying about you and what you're doing. How often do you judge and criticize other people? Maybe a tiny bit but hardly ever? So why then do you assume that everyone is concerned about every little thing you do 24/7?

Furthermore, how do you even know what other people are thinking about you? Unless they tell you, you don't really know what they're thinking. You're not a mind reader are you? Assuming people are judging you negatively is irrational and based on no evidence. You have no idea what someone else is thinking, so if you're going to ASSUME things, why not assume they're thinking well of you or not thinking of you at all?

# Perfectionism: I Let Go of My Need to Be Perfect

Somewhere along the line, I picked up a belief that I needed to 'earn' people's love and friendship. I thought I had to be perfect and amazing in order for anyone to like me because I didn't feel I was enough as I was.

Here is how *Psychology Today* describes perfectionism.

> *For perfectionists, life is an endless report card on accomplishments or looks. It's a fast track to unhappiness, and perfectionism is often accompanied by depression and eating disorders. What makes perfectionism so toxic is that while those in its grip desire success, they are most focused on avoiding failure, so theirs is a negative orientation. Love isn't a refuge; in fact, it feels way too conditional on performance. The need for perfection is usually transmitted in small ways from parents to children, some as silent as a raised eyebrow over a B rather than an A.*[6]

## How Do You Know If You're a Perfectionist?

Do you believe that in order for people to like you, you must always say the right thing? Be funny? Never smell bad? Never make a mistake or appear awkward?

44

Being a perfectionist doesn't mean everything in your life is perfect. It means you think and believe you need to do everything right and be perfect to earn people's acceptance and love. I want you to ask yourself honestly now…

*Do you feel worthy of love and acceptance just because you're you, without having to do anything or earn it?*

If that answer is no, you may be a perfectionist. Perfectionists tend to think in black and white or good or bad terms without leaving any room for grey areas.

*It's either perfect or it's terrible.*

*I have to do everything right or I'm worthless.*

*It's either the best or the worst, no in between.*

They tend to be overly critical of their mistakes and beat themselves up about it. They replay situations where they made mistakes over and over again in their heads. They tend to think that just doing something isn't enough; it has to be done right, and the result MUST be a win. Anything other than success is a total failure. For example, when asking someone on a date, the other person must say yes or it was a total failure, with no acknowledgment or praise given to the courage it took to ask.

Perfectionism is caused by not feeling deep down that you're good enough as you are, so you're always striving to win acceptance—both other people's and your own. You feel you always need to do more to win love and praise.

# The Ways to Overcome Being a Perfectionist Are...

1. Accept that mistakes will happen and everyone makes them; they're a part of life. You don't need to be perfect and never make a mistake to be worthy of love and friendship.
2. Get rid of black and white, perfect or worthless thinking. Accept no-one's perfect and there are grey areas to everything.
3. Focus on the big picture. Does one mistake, awkward conversation or embarrassing moment really matter in the grand scheme of things? Will anyone care or even remember it tomorrow?
4. Celebrate and reward doing rather than achieving perfection. Instead of rewarding yourself only when you do everything perfectly, reward yourself for having the courage to try.
5. Practice looking at yourself the same way that you view others. Do you demand perfection from everyone in your life in order for you to like them?
6. The thing to remember is it doesn't matter how much you do; if you're a perfectionist, it will never be enough. It's a game you can never win. You need to realize you're already enough exactly as you are. You don't need to be perfect for people to like you or accept you, just like you don't need others to be perfect and never make mistakes to like them. You love them for who they are, not how good they are.

## Key Points

1. Remove black and white, perfect or worthless, from your thinking.
2. You don't have to be perfect or do everything right to be worthy of love and acceptance.

46

# *Accept Yourself (Flaws and All)*

The list of things people don't like about themselves is endless: I'm fat, I don't like my nose, my ears are too big, I hate how I'm so introverted, I have a weird-shaped body, etc. Most of the things we dislike about ourselves we don't even have control over. So it's pointless and extremely harmful for your self-esteem to beat yourself up over something that's out of your control, like the way your nose looks.

A good thing to keep in mind is that we all have flaws, every single one of us. No one is perfect, and we all have things we wish to improve about ourselves. Even Hollywood movie stars and models have flaws and things they wish to change about themselves. That's just life. Perfection isn't human, it's an illusion, and even if you had the body or personality of your dreams, you would most likely still become dissatisfied after a while and want more.

Ask most professional bodybuilders and they will tell you they *just* need to gain one more kilo and then they'll be at their perfect weight. Ask most models and they will tell you they *just* need to lose two more pounds. If you get caught up in this type of thinking, it becomes a never-ending quest for perfection that can never be achieved. There is nothing wrong with wanting to improve yourself, but only as long as you don't reject and dislike yourself on the way there.

I want you to make a commitment with me. From now on, we're going to accept ourselves for who we are—good and bad, strengths and weaknesses. You'll never have the confidence you want if you're always putting yourself down, criticizing yourself and judging yourself for your flaws. Self-esteem can only ever come from accepting yourself, flaws and all, and then choosing to love yourself anyway.

*"What I am is how I came out. No one's perfect and you just have to accept your flaws and learn to love yourself."* —Kelly Brook (model & actress)

# I Choose to Feel Good

*"Your relationship with yourself is the most important relationship you'll have in your life. It's the only relationship you have control over. So it makes sense to put the most time into cultivating it."* —Anonymous

Worrying, over-thinking, wanting others to like me, replaying interactions over and over in my head, beating myself up for my flaws, and focusing on all the things I did wrong was just SO MUCH WORK! And it made me feel like crap. It was heavy, it was draining, and it didn't make me feel good.

I now just flat out refuse. Feeling good is more important to me than worrying about what everyone in the room is thinking of me. Feeling good is now more important than replaying that awkward interaction over and over again in my head and feeling hurt over what someone said to me.

Thinking about my flaws doesn't make me feel good and talking about them certainly doesn't. I'm tired of calling myself self-deprecating names like "loser" and feeling inferior around everyone. Being nervous and uncomfortable in public is just far too much effort. I choose to feel good instead. Isn't that what we all desire?

Now please don't misinterpret this. When I say I desire to feel good, it doesn't mean going out and taking drugs to feel good or running away from a situation that scares me. That wouldn't feel good long term. What I mean is I now take better care of my mental state in each moment and make feeling good a priority.

Whatever we accept is exactly what we end up with. Start raising your standards in terms of what mental states you allow to dominate you mind. Choose to feel good as much as you possibly you can. Think of it like giving yourself permission to be emotionally lazy and not wrestling with the heavy draining thoughts that make you feel bad. You do have a choice about what you focus on.

Of course, it's not always that easy to just "feel good," especially in the beginning; but, as with everything I'm teaching you in this book, it gets easier with practice until it becomes a habit. Keep at it, and I promise you'll see results!

To do this successfully requires a shift in how you feel about yourself. It requires you to start believing that you're a worthy person who deserves to feel good no matter what. Don't you think you deserve to feel good? Remember, it's not what we *say* we think but how we *really* think that's important.

Honestly, do you feel you're worthy of feeling good and being happy?

It took me a while to really, truly believe I was worthy of feeling good. I had spent most of my life in a low-vibrational state of either fear, self-loathing, guilt, or shame. I was focusing on all the reasons why I didn't deserve to feel good and because of this, I got more of the same. I had to break out of those negative thought patterns and begin choosing more helpful thoughts.

If you want to feel better about yourself and feel good more often, from now on, no longer allow yourself to focus on thoughts that make you feel like crap. Instead, begin focusing on all the things you like about yourself and all the reasons why you do deserve to be happy. We will talk more about how to do that soon.

## Key Points

1. Become lazy when it comes to negative thinking.
2. Consciously choose to feel good rather than feel bad. It's your choice what you focus on.
3. Raise your standards in terms of what mental states you allow to dominate you mind.

# *Self-Love (I Learned How to Love Myself)*

Growing up, these were some of the phrases I would hear:

*"Don't blow your own trumpet."*
*"Don't be selfish."*
*"Be modest."*
*"He thinks he's so much better than us."*
*"What a bragger."*
*"You're a big shot now, huh?"*

My belief growing up was that it's conceited to love yourself and put your needs first. I should always be modest, never accept a compliment directed at me, and I certainly should never talk about or celebrate my victories—as that would be bragging. I remember the Whitney Houston song, "The Greatest Love of All." I used to laugh at that song and think it was so cheesy. I never understood what she meant until recently; learning to love yourself is indeed the greatest love of all.

I personally believe feeling anxiety (outside of normal situations that warrant anxiety) is the body's way of telling us something needs to change in our lives, kind of like the engine light coming on in your car telling you something isn't right under the hood. The problem is that most of us would rather put some tape over the engine light (mask the symptoms) than to look inside the engine to see what the problem is.

The rate at which I had relief from my depression, social anxiety, general anxiety, OCD and panic attacks was the same rate at which I began to take better care of myself and make my needs a priority in my life. This is what I refer to as self-love. If the term self-love doesn't quite sit well with you, replace it with self-care. They both mean the same thing to me.

I feel there's a massive connection between caring for yourself, respecting yourself, feeling good about yourself, treating yourself well, putting your needs first before tending to others, and the absence of anxiety symptoms.

Many of the great spiritual teachers tell us:

*"You must love yourself first before you can be of service to others."*
*"My cup runneth over."*
*"Put on your own oxygen mask before helping others."*

We'll, the last one is from a flight attendant, but hopefully you get my point. Placing the needs of others before your own leaves you drained and with nothing left to give. In the end, you help no one, including yourself.

What helped me was realizing: *If my cup is not full, if I'm not happy and healthy, if I'm constantly drained, then how can I be of full service to others?* I want to enjoy doing things for others, not feel obligated and drained by it. I always thought loving yourself was kind of narcissistic and weird, but now I understand it's the single most important thing you can do in your life. I'm not talking about being conceited and vain, I'm talking about treating yourself as a someone who is worthy of love and deserves good things.

> *"Love yourself. Forgive yourself. Be true to yourself. How you treat yourself sets the standard for how others will treat you."*
> —Steve Maraboli

Treating myself better wasn't easy in the beginning because of all the limiting beliefs I had. I believed that *it was selfish to put my needs before others*; so, I would feel guilty whenever I put myself first. However, what I found was, when I'm healthy, I can be of more help and give more fully to others. For example, I wouldn't have been able to write this book and help others overcome social anxiety if I hadn't learned self-love and gotten myself healthy. When I'm stuck in anxiety, I'm no fun to be around and certainly not thinking of helping anyone else. So it's less selfish in the long run to put my needs first. When you're healthy and happy, you can be of more service to others. To be healthy and happy, you must look after yourself first before tending to others.

I had to learn to begin using the word *no* and make my needs a priority. For some reason, I really struggled with this. When I did try to start having boundaries with people, it didn't go down too well. They had become used to me being the doormat guy who would do whatever they asked. All of a sudden, I began to say no and they didn't like it one bit. This brought up another false belief—*confrontation is bad*. I began to see how all these beliefs were tied together in an intricate web.

I continued to persevere and make decisions that were right for me, no matter how uncomfortable I felt inside. Over time, it became easier. Each time I said no to something I didn't want to do; my self-esteem would grow a little more. Every time I had the courage to be honest and speak up for myself instead of running from confrontation, my self-esteem would grow even more.

I began to realize that confrontation is a necessary part of life, and it's nothing to be afraid of. As I began to feel better about myself and respect myself, my confidence grew and many of those false beliefs began to fade away. The tank that holds your self-esteem fills back up quite quickly once you patch up those holes it was leaking out from.

## How to Build Self-Worth

At this point in my speech, I usually see people's eyes start to glaze over and they stop paying attention. Most of the people I've worked with have a really hard time accepting they must love themselves no matter what. The tragedy is, the more someone needs a good dose of self-love, the less they feel like doing it. However, once they experience the life changing results first hand, they no longer have a hard time accepting it.

It might feel weird in the beginning to put your needs first and really start to treat yourself well, especially if you're not used to doing it. You may feel that you don't deserve to treat yourself well, or you may feel selfish and conceited. Perhaps you have dependents who rely on you or a lot of responsibilities and you tell yourself you can't put your needs first. If this is the case, what I would ask is; would things really fall apart if you took some more time for yourself? Could you find anyone to help share the workload? Would you be of more service to those you care about if you were happier and healthier?

From my own experience, even if you don't feel like doing nice things for yourself, sometimes you just have to force it and do it anyway. I usually never tell anyone to force anything; but with self-care I make an exception. Initially, I didn't want to do nice things for myself, I didn't feel like I deserved it and I didn't believe it would make any difference.

I had to force it in the beginning to get the ball rolling, then my feelings of self-worth grew and I began *wanting* to treat myself well.

Run an experiment. Do more nice things for yourself for a month or so and see how you feel after the month. Even if you don't feel worthy or it feels weird at first, do it anyway as a trial. You will find that the better you treat yourself, the more you'll believe you're a worthy person and the better you will feel about yourself. It becomes a positive spiral that lifts you out of low self-esteem. Some things you could do are:

One month "put your needs first" policy

One month no self-judgment policy

Long baths and massages

Nice dinners where you order anything you want on the menu

Taking days off work or chores to do whatever you want to do

Movie and shopping days

A weekend away

Listen to your favorite music instead of what everyone else wants to listen to

Cheat days where you eat whatever you want for the day

Spending more time with old friends

Going to the beach, park or lake

Spending time in nature

Quiet time for meditation

Wearing nice clothes that make you feel good

Getting a makeover or new hair style

Reading a good book with a glass of wine

Feel free to add your own favorite pastimes to the list. Do whatever you can to treat yourself better, regardless of whether you feel you deserve it or not. This is how you build feelings of self-worth. Growing self-worth is more of a process of unlearning rather than learning. It's shedding all the hogwash stories you've been telling yourself over the years about why you're not valuable. It's also getting over your need for external praise and validation and going inside for your good feelings. This is what we'll talk about in the next section.

## *I Stopped Looking for My Worth Outside of Myself (Self-Love, Part 2)*

Looking back, I thought the only way I could like myself was if others liked me and praised me. The strange thing was that the more I chased my validation (approval) from external sources, the worse I felt. Other people's praise and validation was like an addiction that I could never get enough of. The high never lasted long, and I kept needing more and more to stop me from crashing. What I really needed to do was go inside for my validation. That's the only place you'll ever get it from.

We have to stop relying on other people to tell us our worth and start relying on ourselves. We'll never find our worth in other people's praise, a sexual partner, our Instagram followers or how many people like us. You and only you are responsible for your own good emotions and happiness. No one else can give you long-term happiness or self-esteem. Sure, when people like you it feels great for a short while, but those good feelings quickly wear off and what happens when they go away? You need more and more or your world starts to fall apart.

*Treasure yourself, love yourself, value yourself. The more you love and accept yourself, the less you need others to like and approve of you. The less you care if others like and approve of you, the less uncomfortable you will feel in social situations. It's all tied to self-love and self-acceptance.*

Learn to see past the smoke and mirrors of fame, wealth and beauty. That famous actor, the CEO of your company, that beautiful woman. None of them is even one iota more deserving of love than you are. No one is above you in the eyes of the creator, not the Queen of England or the President of the United States. Regardless of how some people act, the real truth is we were all created equal. That means we are all valuable and we all have something valuable to contribute to this world. If you didn't, you wouldn't be here. It's no accident that you're here, you are here for a reason. The same goes for your anxiety, it's here to teach you something. I believe anxiety came into my life to teach me how to love and respect myself.

You are valuable. Treat yourself that way, carry yourself that way, speak to yourself that way. Hold your head up high, and be proud of who you are. Don't beat yourself up anymore; become your own best friend and constantly give yourself kind words of encouragement.

Even if you've been treating yourself like dirt your whole life, today you can start a new chapter and decide to love yourself.

> *"Our deepest fear is not that we are inadequate. Our deepest fear is that we are powerful beyond measure. It is our light, not our darkness that most frightens us. We ask ourselves, Who am I to be brilliant, gorgeous, talented, and fabulous? Actually, who are*

*you not to be? You are a child of God. Your playing small does not serve the world. There is nothing enlightened about shrinking so that other people will not feel insecure around you. We are all meant to shine, as children do. We were born to make manifest the glory of God that is within us. It is not just in some of us; it is in everyone and as we let our own light shine, we unconsciously give others permission to do the same. As we are liberated from our own fear, our presence automatically liberates others."*
-Marianne Williamson

## Key Points

1. Putting yourself first isn't selfish. Your cup needs to be full before you can give to others.
2. Learning to love yourself and treat yourself well is the single most important thing you can do in your life, not just for yourself but all those in your life. When you're healthy and happy, everyone benefits.
3. Let go of your need for external approval and go within; that's the only place you'll ever find it. You'll never find your self-worth outside of yourself.

## *Unhelpful Beliefs (Knock Out the Kingpins and the Rest Will Fall)*

Here are the main beliefs and things I used to tell myself that led to me being anxious around people. Even if I didn't directly tell myself these things, deep down, they're what I believed. Every action I took or didn't take was because of one of these beliefs. Like a big ball of tangled string, when I began to pick away at a few loose ends and challenge them as false, the whole thing began to unravel. See if you can relate to any of these.

## I Had a Belief That I Was Worthless.

I didn't think I was worth very much. In fact, I thought poop had more value than I did. Nobody ever really told me I was valuable or meant anything to them and because I was always looking for others to show me what my worth was, I ended up hating myself. I would let people walk all over me and actually expected it because that's what I thought I deserved.

## I Had a Belief That I Was Inferior to Just about Everyone.

If you believe you're inferior to others, how does that make you act? It means you think everyone is above you and better than you, so what they say is more important than what you say.

It means you think they're important and, therefore, their approval is important. You had better be on your best behavior around those people because you don't want them to judge you negatively. Thinking people are superior to you is bound to make you feel anxious around them.

## I Had a Belief That Everyone Everywhere Was Judging Me Negatively All the Time.

When I was around people, I wouldn't talk much. I was constantly monitoring and censoring my words and actions because I didn't want to say something stupid and be made fun of.

## I Believed Confrontation Was Bad and Must Be Avoided at All Costs.

I wouldn't stand up for myself and tell people no, as I was trying to avoid any kind of confrontation at all costs. Not a helpful belief if you want to be happy or become more socially confident.

## I Believed That Everyone Had to Like Me.

This belief made me want to agree with everyone, flatter them, and say things I didn't really mean. I would do things that weren't right by me in order to gain others' acceptance.

## I Believed in Order for People to Like Me, I Must Be Perfect and Do Everything They Ask of Me.

I believed in order for others to like me, I must never smell bad, I must never say the wrong thing, and I must always give them my full, undivided attention. This is the perfectionist thinking we talked about.

## I Believed If I Ever Did Anything Wrong or Told Someone No, I Would Be Rejected.

When I thought about standing up for myself, my mind would race to catastrophe, and I would picture a scene where no one in the world liked me and I lived out the rest of my days alone. (Honestly, I would do this.) All because I told someone no or disagreed.

Here are some more false things I used to believe and tell myself. Do any of these sound familiar to you?

*"I'm shy."*
*"I'm just not a confident, person; I was born this way."*
*"I'm not funny."*
*"I can't help it; it's just the way I am."*
*"I have social anxiety, so that's why I can't go out and meet people."*
*"I have a chemical imbalance in my brain."*
*"I'm an introvert, and introverts are naturally shy."*
*"Things are always going to be like this; might as well get used to it."*
*"What's the point of even trying?"*
*"Why me? Life isn't fair."* (I loved that one.)

*"He's better looking than me so he deserves love and I don't."*
*"I'm ugly."*
*"I'm not good with women."*
*"I'm not a people person."*
*"Most people are mean and unkind."*
*"I must always put others first."*
*"Some people are more important than me."*
*"I have to be nice to everyone."*
*"Confrontation is bad."*
*"I should never say no to a request that I can do."*

## What Is a Belief?

As Tony Robbins says,

*"A belief is nothing but a feeling of certainty about what something means."*

A belief is an idea or theory you hold in your mind that you perceive to be a fact. The funny thing is, something doesn't have to be true for you to believe it. People believed the world was flat for centuries but it didn't make it true. I'm sure you currently have many negative things you believe about yourself that are not fact. In this section, we are going to challenge them together.

## How Are Negative Beliefs Formed?

A belief is formed through:

1. *Past experiences that you have given meaning to.* For example, being chosen last at the school dance and thinking it means everyone thinks you're ugly.
2. *Someone else telling you something (including news, media, magazines and authority figures).* For example, someone telling you that you're ugly, either directly to your face or via subtle suggestion on TV or in magazines.

3. *Telling yourself something.* For example, looking in the mirror and telling yourself you're ugly.

The more you, or someone whose opinion you consider to be valid, tells you something, the more you will believe it. This has actually been proven. That's why it is so important that we stop repeatedly telling ourselves hurtful, negative things and also stop listening to the negative things others say about us.

Negative beliefs about ourselves are mainly formed from past experiences when we were children.

## Here are some examples:

You might have been punished, neglected, smacked, or abandoned as a child and now you believe you're worthless and you deserve that kind of treatment.

Your parents, loved ones and teachers may have told you hurtful things when they were mad. Things like, "You're a bad kid," "You'll never amount to anything," "You're just like your father," etc. Now you have come to believe these things.

Perhaps you got smacked and punished when your parents or teachers were mad at you. Now you believe you must always keep people happy or pain will come to you.

Maybe you were told to "never talk back" and "don't argue." If you did, you got punished. Now you believe confrontation is bad and should be avoided it at all costs.

Perhaps your parents or teachers were always telling you to "be quiet" or "shut up." If you talked too much or stood out in class, you got punished. Now "being quiet" in social situations is your survival strategy to avoid pain.

Your parents may have also said things about the world such as, "Never trust or talk to strangers," "People can't be trusted," etc. Now you have come to distrust and fear people.

If you ever told your parents or authority figures no, pain would come in the form of punishment. So you may now believe you must never tell anyone no or there will be pain.

You might have been told you're ugly, fat, unlikeable, uncool etc., by friends or other school kids. Now you believe you're unattractive, 'less than,' or inferior to others and don't deserve to be loved.

Maybe you felt, or were told, you were "not as confident as other kids" or "not as smart," and you have come to believe it.

If you didn't like the same things that everyone else liked, maybe you were told there was something wrong with you. This might have lead you to believe, you're weird, different, odd or inferior.

If your parents (or other family members) rarely acknowledged your good points and always focused on your mistakes and weakness, this may have led to the belief you're not good enough. It may have also led you to believe you need to be perfect and do everything right to be loved.

## Negative Beliefs Can Also Come From:

*Opinions from authority figures:* For example, being told by someone you trust that you'll be on medication for life, you were born shy, you have a learning disability, or you have a genetic fault in your brain. Now you believe what they have told you because you consider them to be in a position of authority and they know better than you.

*Comparing yourself to other people:* Feeling inferior if you don't measure up to other people's results or looks. Looking at magazines of photoshopped models or men on steroids and feeling bad about yourself. Comparing yourself to confident people who've had years of social experience and because you don't currently have the same skills, you believe it means there is something inherently wrong with you.

*An abusive relationship:* Making someone else's actions toward you mean something about your worth as a person.

*Being cheated on:* Believing it was your fault because you were cheated on and it means something about your worth as a person or your looks.

*Growing up poor:* Perhaps you feel inferior to people because of your financial history or you inherited your parents' negative beliefs about money and the world.

*Criticism and judgement from others:* Accepting other people's negative opinions about you as facts and not challenging them or questioning their validity and the motivations behind them. Perhaps others were jealous of you or feeling insecure, so they had to try and bring you down in order to feel better about themselves.

## How Do We Change a Limiting Belief?

Beliefs are so powerful, they can either be your greatest ally or your worst enemy. Beliefs act like self-fulfilling prophecies; whatever you believe about yourself, you'll see evidence of.

For example, if you believe you're ugly, your brain will only look for evidence that confirms your belief and filter out any contradictory evidence. You'll only focus on the parts of yourself you don't like, totally dismissing your good points. The worst part is, anytime someone tells you that you do look nice, you'll reject the compliment, thinking they're being either sarcastic or insincere.

However, if you believe you're attractive, your brain will only focus on your good points, and anytime someone gives you a compliment, you believe them, thus confirming your belief that you're attractive.

It's the same with being shy. If you believe you're shy, your mind will filter out all the times you weren't shy and only remember the times you were, thus confirming your belief.

So, in knowing this, it's actually easier than you think to change a negative belief you hold about yourself, even if you've had it your entire life. You simply change what you focus on. Instead of choosing to focus on the negative experiences and memories that confirm your negative belief, you now choose to focus on the evidence that contradicts the limiting belief. Then you go about creating new positive reference experiences to confirm your more empowering belief.

There are always two sides to every story; just because you believe something doesn't mean it's true. I believed I was ugly my whole life; now I believe I'm attractive. I'm still the same person and I have plenty of evidence to support both. The difference is, now I choose to focus on the evidence that supports the belief I want to have.

## Beliefs Exercise #1

The first step to changing your negative beliefs is to list as accurately as possible some of the things you believe about yourself, who you are and what you're capable of. In what ways have you been putting yourself down and criticizing yourself? What have others told you in your life that you believed?

Go ahead now and write down all the negative things you believe about yourself and the world before reading any further.

# *Reframing Negative Beliefs*

Changing our negative beliefs is one of the most important parts of overcoming social anxiety and growing self-esteem. Just like how other people's opinions about you are not facts, that also applies to your own negative opinions about yourself.

It's up to us to challenge our negative beliefs, and we do this by becoming like a scientist and using critical thinking. Remember, your beliefs are not the truth. They are simply a theory you currently hold about yourself or the world. So we will act like a scientist and set out to disprove our negative theories.

## Beliefs Exercise #2

Once you have listed as many negative beliefs about yourself as you can think of, the next thing to do is run each belief through these questions...

1. *Is this belief I have of myself an opinion or a proven fact?*
2. *Is it possible this belief is not the truth?*
3. *What is the evidence for this belief?*
4. *What is the evidence against this belief?*
5. *Is this belief helping me?*
6. *Are there any positives in me or past situations that I am ignoring?*
7. *Is it possible that people in my life really did love me and think I was valuable but they just didn't know how to show it very well?*
8. *Is it possible other people's opinions of me may not be correct or valid?*
9. *Is it possible I've only been looking for the negative and overlooking some of the positive evidence about myself?*

# Beliefs Exercise #3

Once I ran all my beliefs through those questions, I then replaced them with more empowering beliefs. Here are some reframes I used instead.

*"I'm worthless and inferior."* Became, *"There's not one person out there who is any more deserving of love than me. We are all equal. Sure there are people with great skills and looks, but that doesn't make them any better than me."*

*"Everyone everywhere is judging me negatively all the time."* Became, *"People have their own lives and flaws to be concerned about; they're not judging me and what I'm doing, just as I'm not judging them."*

*"Everyone has to like me."* Became, *"Not everyone has to like me, just like I don't have to like everyone. It only matters that I like me."*

*"In order for people to like me, I must be perfect and do everything they ask of me."* Became, *"Do I treat others this way? Do others need to be perfect and do everything I ask for me to like them?"*

*"If I tell someone no, I will be rejected."* Became, *"People say no all the time. It's totally normal and people respect someone with boundaries."*

*"I'm shy."* Became, *"Up until this point, I've chosen avoidance and shy behaviors, but, in this moment, I will choose a new way of acting."*

*"I'm just not a confident person. I was born this way."* Became, *"That's not true; I remember times in my life when I felt confident. Confidence will come the more I believe it."*

*"I'm not a funny person."* Became, *"I remember times when I made people laugh; actually, I can be funny."*

*"I can't help it; it's just the way I am."* Became, *"I can be anyone I choose to be. Other people have overcome much worse conditions than mine."*

*"I have social anxiety, so that's why I can't go out and meet people."* Became, *"I'm no longer willing to let this label control my life. Social anxiety is not a life sentence. I can be whoever I want to be. I'm no longer willing to let this social anxiety stop me from being happy."*

*"I have a chemical imbalance in my brain, and that's why I have anxiety."* Became, *"Is it possible I'm doing things that are contributing to my anxiety and it's not genetic? I know I have the ability to heal myself and live a life free of anxiety. Anxiety isn't my natural state of being."*

*"I'm an introvert, and introverts are shy and just like to be by themselves."* Became, *"There are many introverts who are confident and enjoy socializing. They just also need their alone time to recharge their batteries; it's not an excuse to be a hermit."*

*"What's the point? Things are always going to be like this; I might as well get used to it."* Became, *"I will not live a mediocre life anymore; I'm no longer willing to settle for anything less. I am capable of change and I will do whatever it takes to live the life of my dreams."*

*"Why me? It's not fair."* Became, *"This is my journey and lessons I have to learn. Now, I'm going to choose a new story for myself—a story of triumph, not misery."*

*"If I'm not perfect, I'm worthless."* Became, *"No one is perfect; we all make mistakes sometimes, and it's okay."*

*"He's better looking than me."* Became, *"I will not compare myself to others; we're all on our own journey."*

*"I'm ugly."* Became, *"I'm the way I am. There were a lot of times in my life when people told me I looked good, and I'm exercising hard to improve my body and health."*

*"I'm not confident around women."* Became, *"Only because I haven't had much practice. I know if I put my mind to it and work on it, I will improve like I have in other areas of my life."*

*"I'm not a people person."* Became, *"There have been times when I've enjoyed socializing and been good at it."*

*"Most people are mean and unkind."* Became, *"Is it possible that I've just been focusing on the bad? What about all the great and kind people I've met?"*

*"I must always put others first."* Became, *"You can't please everyone; you must love yourself first before you can be of service to others."*

*"Some people are more important than me."* Became, *"No one in the world is any more important than anyone else; we're all equal in God's eyes."*

*"I should be nice to everyone."* Became, *"Being nice is great, but it's more important to be yourself than to be nice or liked."*

*"Confrontation is bad."* Became, *"Confrontation is a necessary and normal part of life; it can't be avoided and more harm comes when you try to avoid it than face it."*

*"I should never say no to a request that I can do."* Became, *"You need to care for yourself before you can be of any major help to others; your cup must be full."*

Go ahead and do the same with some of your negative and disempowering beliefs. Reframe them with something more positive, empowering and truthful.

*\* If you would like some more help with getting rid of your limiting beliefs and raising your self-esteem, please check out my in-depth online program at www.socialanxietyacademy.com.*

# The Deadly "I'm" Disease

A lot of the previously mentioned beliefs weren't obvious to me at the time. For my whole teens and twenties, I didn't even realize I had most of them. Either someone else pointed them out for me, or I read about them in books like you're doing now. The reason I didn't notice them for so long was because of the labels I had placed on myself.

We touched on this subject earlier, but I want to go into it a little more deeply here. I believed I was born shy and naturally lacked confidence and there was nothing I could do to fix it. So instead of looking for the real causes of my social anxiety, I blamed something out of my control like genetics, assumed I could do nothing about it, and, therefore, did nothing about it. You're not ruled by your genetics. You can overcome a tendency to want to be introverted and shy by living a healthy active lifestyle and thinking healthy thoughts.

Once I removed the "I was born shy" I saw some painful facts. What I hadn't been able to see was that every time I believed what someone else said about me, every time I didn't stand up for myself, every time I self-rejected, every time I made other people more important than me, and every time I called myself horrible names, my self-esteem would dip a little lower. Eventually, I had no self-esteem left and the vicious cycle continued. I went on believing I was born shy and not confident, not realizing it was my self-rejecting behaviors and negative beliefs that were causing it all along.

Be careful when using "I haves" or "I ams." If what comes after is positive, such as "I am confident," then it's one of the most helpful things you can say. However, if what comes after is negative, such as "I am shy," you've just boxed yourself in and made it almost impossible for you to act in any way other than shy.

## Key Points

1. It's so important to stop blaming things that are out of your control. Get rid of the "I am" labels and see if there's anything you're doing that may be contributing to your anxiety and shyness.
2. Using negative "I ams" boxes you in and makes it almost impossible to act in other ways.

# Reminder: Remember What You're Playing For

At this point, you may feel overwhelmed and think, *Do I really have to do all of this work?*

Yes, I know making lists and analyzing yourself is mentally draining and annoying. I know there will be times you want to skip these exercises, as I did, but remember what you're playing for.

Your happiness is literally on the line here, every day you spend unfulfilled and nervous around people is a day you'll never get back.

# It's Not the Event That Hurts: It's the Meaning We Give to the Event

It has been said, it's not the event that causes the anxiety, it's the interpretation and meaning we give to the event. Two people can have identical experiences on a roller coaster and one loves it while the other is terrified and hates it.

Two people can ask someone on a date and get rejected. One person laughs it off and says, "There are plenty more fish in the sea," while the other vows, "I'll never do that again for as long as I live." The rejection itself doesn't hurt otherwise both people would be hurt; it's the meaning we give to the rejection. One person doesn't take it personally, but the other makes it mean something about their worth as a person.

Following on from the previous beliefs exercise, we need to start digging into the underlying irrational beliefs and assumptions we have about a certain situation that scares us. This is a very helpful CBT (cognitive behavioral therapy) self-analysis technique I used to help me start putting things into perspective.

It goes like this…

Thought: *Even though I'm lonely and want a partner, I'm too scared to ask my crush out on a date.*

Why?

*Well, what if I asked her out and she said no? It would really hurt and be embarrassing.*

Why would it hurt or be embarrassing?

*Because it would make me feel bad about myself. It would mean she thinks I'm not attractive and not good enough to date someone like her.*

Why would it be bad if I'm unattractive?

*Then no one would want to date me, and I'll always be alone and miserable.*

There are many assumptions and irrational conclusions here:

1. Because someone said no to my date request, it means they think I'm ugly and not good enough.
2. Because one person may think I'm ugly, everyone must think I'm ugly.
3. I have to be good looking to be worthy of having a relationship.
4. Because one person said no, I'm not good enough for anyone.

Something along these lines is the underlying thought process most of us have when we contemplate asking someone out or talking to someone we find attractive. Of course, we're not always aware of this; we just get an instant feeling of fear and nervousness. But when we dig deeper, we find these irrational beliefs are causing the fear. We need to challenge these false beliefs to see that they're not serving us.

The next process would be to cross-examine yourself to find the truth.

*Q)* Is it true that because someone didn't want to go on a date with me, it means they think I'm ugly and not good enough?

*A) Well, no, it could be a number of reasons. Maybe they have a partner, or they just broke up, or they're too busy.*

*Q)* Is it true that because one person may think I'm ugly, everyone must think I'm ugly?

*A) Well, no, I think some people are attractive while my friends don't. Everyone has different tastes in people.*

*Q)* Is it true that because one person said no, I'm not good enough for anyone?

*A) Well, no, there are billions of people out there, all with different likes and tastes. What one person likes, another doesn't.*

*Q)* Is it true that because one person said no, I'm not worthy of having a relationship?

*A) No, I guess not, it doesn't really mean anything about me.*

The final process would be asking if it would really matter if it didn't go well?

*Q)* Would it really matter if they said they didn't want to go on a date with me?

*A) It would be better if they said yes, but I will still be okay even if they don't and I will feel great about myself for asking. I guess when I think of it like that, I have much more to gain than to lose.*

## Your Turn

I want you to write down things that scare you and complete the above process; it will help immensely to put your fears into perspective.

Some examples would be:

Speaking up at school/work or sharing your ideas

Asking someone for help or directions

Starting your own business or asking for a raise

Going to a party you want to go to

So the process would go like this...

1.  Start with *I'm feeling anxiety about xyz....*
2.  Ask yourself why two or three times to get to the underlying beliefs and assumptions causing the anxiety.
3.  Cross-examine the beliefs and assumptions to prove their truthfulness and challenge them with the truth.
4.  Ask would you still be ok if the worst happened.

# I Stopped Taking Things So Personally (Not Everything Is about Me)

I used to take everything that happened to me so personally. If someone cut me off mid-sentence, it meant I was boring. If someone snapped at me, it meant they didn't like me. If someone didn't answer my phone call, they were mad at me or didn't like me anymore. What helped me was realizing not everything is about me. We all have bad days—people have bad moods and sometimes people snap under stress—and maybe you happen to be in the line of fire. Sometimes, people say hurtful things to you that they don't really mean when they're stressed, angry and frustrated. Or they may be really busy and don't have time to answer your call or reply to your text. It doesn't mean you've done something wrong or they don't like you anymore.

The next time someone criticizes you, snaps at you, ignores you, or doesn't reply to your text, don't take it personally. You don't know what kind of day they've had. Maybe they got a parking ticket or found out some bad news. They may be tired or anxious themselves, in a hurry, or hungry. It could be a number of things. Now, before I get angry or upset with someone and take it personally, I assume that something like that has happened and know it has nothing to do with me.

# *Watch Your Mouth! (I Worked on My Self-Talk until My Worst Enemy Became My Best Friend)*

HEY! Do I have your attention? Good, because I'm going to share with you what I consider to be the #1 cause of poor self-esteem and social anxiety. That is, the way we talk to ourselves, aka, self-talk.

We all have a little voice in our heads constantly talking to us. Some people refer to it as our internal dialogue. The things we tell ourselves have a very powerful effect on the way we feel about ourselves and what we believe is possible for us. Whatever you speak into existence and give your attention to eventually becomes your reality, so it's really important to pay attention to what you're telling yourself.

Here's a little list of things I would tell myself on a daily basis:

"Why are you so stupid?"

"OMG, I can't do anything right; I'm such a loser!"

"WTF is wrong with you, Tobi?"

"I can't help it; I'll never change."

"Everyone at this party is going to hate me."

"Whoa! You *are* ugly; no wonder you're single."

"I can't even do this one thing right."

"Everyone thinks you're ridiculous."

"Why are you so weak and emotional?"

"I should be better; I should have done things differently."

"How do you ever expect to have a girlfriend if you can't even talk without getting nervous?"

The way you talk to yourself speaks volumes about how you feel about yourself on the inside. Can you see how telling myself these things may have led to my poor self-esteem and anxiety around others? Looking back now, I would never say to my worst enemy the things I said to myself. I WAS my own worst enemy.

Is your inner voice your best friend or worst critic?

Chances are, if you're not feeling socially confident, you have some negative self-talk going on. What are some of the things you tell yourself when you're in a social interaction or while you're going about your day?

Are you supportive, encouraging, and praising? Or are you harsh, critical, and judgmental of yourself? What do you say to yourself before you're about to go for a job interview? Do you say to yourself something like the following?

"I'm great at my job. I'd be an asset to any company; of course, they're going to hire me!"

Or do you say something along the lines of this?

"You suck. You're not good enough; you're not smart enough for this job. You don't deserve to make more money."

What about when you're thinking about talking to someone you find attractive?

Do you tell yourself something like?

"I'm a nice person. I know I have a lot to offer and would make someone really happy."

Or do you say something along the lines of this?

"Whoa, what are you doing? You're not good enough for him/her; they're out of your league. You're too ugly/fat/shy/(insert put down here). Forget about it, there's no point. You have no chance."

Again, none of what I'm saying in this book is ever meant to make you feel bad about yourself. I'm telling you this to point out there are things here we need to change if we want to improve our self-esteem and our lives. You will never fully be able to stop this critical voice, but what I do now is make a conscious effort to catch myself in the process of having a negative thought, realize it's not the truth, and reframe it.

For example, I would be at a party and see people looking in my direction and laughing. My self-talk would go like this...

*"They're all laughing at me. It's probably my clothes. I knew I shouldn't have worn this shirt. They all think I'm ugly; they're laughing at how ugly I am. Yeah, I must be ugly."*

I began to catch myself every time I could see I was going on one of my downward spirals. Most of your self-talk is probably happening to you on autopilot. The first step is becoming aware that you're actually doing it; the next step is to challenge it with a rational thought.

First, I became aware and labeled it.

*"Okay, here's my self-talk telling me that I'm ugly again."*

Then I challenged it by asking myself something logical such as.

*"How can I be sure they're laughing at me? Am I a mind reader? Maybe someone told a funny joke and they just happened to be looking my way. Anyway, what they think about me doesn't concern me; it only matters how I feel about myself."*

After this, I immediately thought.

*"My only concern is that I feel good; I don't feel like participating in any more of this negativity. It's just not fun and doesn't feel good."*

Becoming aware of your self-talk is a gradual process but it does get easier with practice. Most of my negative thinking was subconscious. I wasn't even aware I was doing it most of the time. However, when I became conscious of these thoughts I could begin to catch them.

From now on, make an effort to no longer talk down to yourself and be your own worst enemy. Don't feel bad about yourself if you slip up sometimes. We all do. Initially, you probably won't be able to do much to stop your negative thoughts. Chances are, they've become subconscious thought patterns. Depending on how often and long you've been using negative self-talk, you'll perhaps start off only being able to catch one out of five of them.

Over time, as long as you stay focused and aware, you'll find yourself noticing more and more of this negative self-talk as it comes up. After a while, it will become less and less frequent. Never expect it to stop completely, but now you have the tools to challenge it or not pay attention to it anymore. Remember, everyone in the world has a little voice in their head telling them why they're not capable, or ugly, or worthless, etc. The difference is some choose not to pay attention to it because they know it's not the truth.

I highly recommend you read up on the law of attraction. Most of you are probably familiar with it already. The premise of the LOA is: "You get and become what you think about and focus on." Studying law of attraction literature helped me become more aware of the creative power of my thoughts and to be on guard for any negative self-talk. You become what you think about, so train yourself to think and say good things about yourself.

## Key Points

1. Don't let yourself get sucked into the negative spiral of these thoughts anymore. Choose to feel good instead.
2. Become aware of your negative self-talk and challenge it with a rational, more helpful thought or chose not to pay attention to it.
3. You become what you think about and focus on, so train yourself to think only helpful thoughts.

## *Your Thoughts Are Not You*

My whole life, I've struggled with a form of obsessive compulsive disorder called obsessive and intrusive thoughts. It's the O part of OCD. What this means is my mind will show me all kinds of weird and horrible things, usually my greatest fears. I used to really beat myself up about the type of weird thoughts I had. Again, beating myself up about it never made me feel better, only worse.

I thought I was the only one in the world who had negative and weird thoughts. My therapist really helped me with this. He made me aware that thinking a wide range of thoughts is common and there's nothing wrong with me. People have weird, wonderful, and wacky thoughts all the time.

If you struggle with negative thoughts about yourself that you'd rather not have, you're not alone, and there's nothing wrong with you. Next time you get a thought you don't like, try not to bite into it; just let it flow right on through. Think of your thoughts like a big buffet at a restaurant. There are all kinds of food available, some good for you and others not so good for you. You have the choice of what thoughts you'll put on your plate; you don't have to bite into a harmful thought just because it's being served at the buffet. You don't always have a choice of what's being served in the buffet of your mind, but you always have the choice of what you bite into.

I want you to know that you are not your thoughts, no matter how weird or negative you might think they are. You may constantly have thoughts that you're a loser or ugly or worthless, but like we talked about earlier, just because you think something doesn't make it the truth.

I don't know why we think the things we do, but I do know it doesn't say anything about who we are or whether we're good people. Meditating really helps with thinking less, and I'm going to discuss that later.

## Predicting the Future (Worst-Case Scenario Thinking)

When we think about a future event, we tend to picture it as a movie in our minds. If I asked you to picture where you want to go for your next vacation, there would probably be a little movie or a series of images running in your mind about the trip there, the beach, and sipping cocktails in the sun.

Worst-case scenario thinking (aka predicting the future or catastrophizing) is picturing a future event and expecting the worst will happen, or expecting the worst possible outcome for yourself in a situation. When you think about going to a party, do you see yourself having a good time? Or do you picture yourself feeling uncomfortable and all your conversations being awkward?

What about before a job interview or giving a presentation at work or school? Do you see it going well for you or do you picture yourself stuttering your words and it going terribly?

When we lack confidence in something, our brains want to rush into worst-case scenario thinking and picture all the terrible things that would happen to us if we failed. Most of these will never happen or get blown way out of proportion. WCST will stop you in your tracks. Don't let yourself go down that route anymore; you know where it will lead you. Again, keep in mind most of this will probably be happening on autopilot (subconsciously) and you may not even realize you're doing it. For me, I didn't even know I was doing it for years until I was made aware, and I still catch myself doing it now sometimes.

YOU DO HAVE A CHOICE!

Along with your self-talk, become aware when you're having one of your bad episodes (as I like to call them) and then you can do something about them. Once we RECOGNIZE these thoughts, we can begin to stop paying attention to them. You need to develop the habit of catching these thoughts as they pop up. Sometimes, they'll originate as a voice in your head (self-talk) like, "This party is going to suck. No one will want to talk to me, and I'll be there standing by myself in the corner." Then the negative movies will begin to play of how you expect the situation to turn out. This is immediately followed by fear and anxiety in the body.

At first, it will be hard to catch yourself during one of these negative movies. But as you get better, you'll catch more and more of them. It will take some conscious effort in the beginning, but eventually, you'll form a habit of catching them and choosing to play a more positive outcome in your mind. This will be life changing for you.

# *Introspection Checkpoint*

Now that we're quite deep into the book and I've shared some key concepts with you, if you haven't done so already, I'd like you to now have a look at how these concepts may relate to your own life and circumstances.

Based on what we've talked about so far, have you been able to identify some of the reasons why you may be feeling anxious or shy around people? Can you identify some of the habits and behaviors that may be causing your low self-esteem?

Are you self-rejecting? Beating yourself up for having social anxiety? Acting like someone you're not? Afraid of confrontation and telling people no? Telling yourself hurtful things and always putting yourself down? Placing other people's needs above your own? Are you "should-ing" yourself? Taking things too personally? Do you believe you must be perfect to be liked? Are you looking for your worth in the approval of other people instead of yourself? Do you believe you must never appear weak or emotional in front of other people? Do you believe if you do appear anxious, it means you're a weak person?

Have a long introspection about these questions because it's really important to first identify, then get rid of these limiting beliefs and behaviors that are holding you back.

Here are some helpful things to remember:

*"You're not here to live up to anyone else's expectations."*

*"You're not here on this Earth to please others."*
*"It doesn't matter what anyone else thinks of you, as long as you like who you are."*
*"You don't have to explain yourself to anyone."*
*"You don't need to impress anyone."*
*"You don't need to compare yourself to anyone."*
*"Disapproval, haters, and judgmental people will always be there. Get used to it; that's just the way things are."*
*"It's okay if someone doesn't agree with you."*
*"It's okay if someone tells you no, and it's okay to say no to others."*
*"It's okay to be awkward or say something silly every now and again; no one is perfect."*
*"It's okay to not perform exactly how you wanted; no one is perfect."*
*"The people you think are judging you have just as many problems, flaws, and insecurities as you have."*

And finally, a famous quote by Bernard M. Baruch:

*"Be who you are and say what you feel because those who mind don't matter, and those who matter don't mind."*

# *The Man in the Mirror (Self-Image)*

Your self-image is the perception you have about yourself and all you're capable of. We all have a self-image. How we are at our jobs, how we are as friends, socially, at sports, in relationships, and where we stand in relation to others. Your self-image isn't only shaped by the experiences you've had in the past but also your interpretation of those experiences. People with social anxiety and poor self-esteem tend to have a poor self-image. They tend to see themselves as shy, unconfident, and inferior to others.

It's really hard to outperform your self-image. Some would say it's almost impossible. How you see yourself on the inside will govern the results you get on the outside; so, it's of the utmost importance that you change your self-image to that of someone who is socially confident. If you continue to see yourself as shy and inferior (or whatever else it is for you) on the inside, you'll keep getting those results on the outside.

## What Factors Contribute to a Poor Self-Image?

A poor self-image is created by focusing only on your flaws and failures and seeing yourself for less than you truly are instead of focusing on your good points. It's formed by seeing yourself and your accomplishments as average and other people's as much better—seeing yourself as inferior to others, either because other people have been telling you this your whole life or from your own flawed perception of yourself and events. An example would be having a few awkward conversations, then telling yourself you're an awkward person.

It can also come from constantly putting yourself down, calling yourself names such as *loser* and *idiot* when you fail and from taking other people's negative opinions about you on board as your opinion of yourself.

A few years ago, if you had asked me what my self-image was, it would have gone something like this.

*"I'm a twenty-eight-year-old from Australia. I'm shy, introverted, and not good with people. That's just the way I was born. I'm not really a people person and I prefer to be by myself. I'm good at sports, especially surfing and making music. I feel I have above average intelligence. I'm terrible with women. I feel we're on different planets and they never even see me. They always end up with confident jerks who are smooth talkers, and I'm not a smooth talker. I'm not happy with how I look. I'm too skinny, I have a weird looking face, my ears are too big, and I look like I'm a teenager even though I'm twenty-eight."*

Can you see how holding an image like this of myself may have been affecting my self-esteem? Remember what I said before about how our beliefs filter out any contradictory evidence? Anything that didn't match up with my self-image was rejected and I only looked for situations that confirmed how I *already* felt about myself. This is known as confirmation bias, when you only seek out evidence that supports what you already believe, and you disregard the rest. We need to stop doing it if we want to change our self-image.

*In a minute, I'll get you to write down your current self-image.*

## How Do We Improve Our Self-Image?
First, we choose to turn our attention to the good things we like about ourselves rather than our flaws and all the things we don't like. Then, we remember all the times we did well and only focus on those instead of remembering all the times we messed up or someone has put us down.

The third step is to form an image of the person you want to be and visualize that person in your mind constantly. How does she/he think, speak, walk, act, and relate to others?

The final step is to begin taking action to become that confident person we see in our minds (which we will talk about a little later).

We always try to act in line with how we see ourselves on the inside; when we don't, it feels very weird to us and can cause quite a lot of stress and mental discomfort. You may have heard stories about people who lost a lot of weight and put it right back on again. They may look skinny on the outside after their diet, but their self-image is still that of a fat person. Unless they change their self-image, the weight is likely to come back. Another example of this is people who win the lottery and are broke again in a year. Their self-image is still that of a poor person.

Your self-image has an extremely powerful effect on your life; a negative self-image can be disastrous to your success. If we see ourselves as the shy type, it will feel very strange for us to act in any other way. This is another reason why we stay trapped in shyness our whole lives; it feels weird and inauthentic to act confident when we see ourselves as shy. We feel as though we're lying to ourselves.

In the beginning, when I was just starting to break out of my shell and act more confident, I would feel like a phony. My mind would say, *"Why are you acting like this? This isn't you."* I felt like someone was about to walk over and say, *"Hey, loser! You're not confident; go back and stand in the corner where you belong."*

This is what I mean when I say it's going to feel weird when you begin acting in new ways that are different to how you see yourself. You'll feel like everyone can see through you and call you out for being a fake. But others can't see through you and they don't know how you're feeling on the inside; they'll respond to exactly how you're coming across. If you're coming across as confident, they'll accept you as confident and not question it, not even for a second.

The most important thing is to not let the initial weirdness stop you. Your self-image will catch up as long as you keep at it and keep acting as the person you want to be. Visualization really helped with overcoming those feelings of being a faker, and I will explain how to do that in the next section.

Right now, though, chances are your current self-image needs to be updated; so, I'm going to give you some exercises.

## *Self-Image Exercise*

In this exercise, what you're going to do is take a look at your life and examine who you THINK you are in each area.

I want you to write down who you think you are in the following areas:

*In your career?*
*How much money are you worthy of making?*
*What kind of partner are you capable of attracting?*
*What kind of friend are you?*
*How smart are you?*
*How attractive are you?*
*How are you with the opposite sex?*
*How are you in social settings and with people?*

Don't sugar coat it, but don't make it worse than it is either; just be totally honest with yourself. Who do you really, deep down, think you are at all these important things?

Please take some time to do that now.

Now, if you have any parts of your self-image you're not happy with, I want you to re-examine them. When was the last time you tested these assumptions and where did they come from?

*Because someone else told you so?*
*Because it has always been like that?*
*Because you failed in the past?*
*Because you stopped trying after a few bad experiences?*

Remember, we're constantly growing and becoming better every day. If any part of your self-image isn't what you want it to be, perhaps it time to start re-examining some of these assumptions you hold about yourself. In the next section, we'll talk about visualization and how that can supercharge your self-image makeover.

## Key Points

1. Your self-image determines your results. Focus only on your good points and remember only your wins.
2. Stop focusing on your flaws and weaknesses.

# *Visualization: The Blueprint to Becoming the Person You Want to Be*

I've talked about visualization a bit in this book already. If you're not familiar with visualization, it simply means, picturing yourself performing a task in your mind. I use visualization on a daily basis. I really think it has been key in helping me achieve my goals and become more confident.

When we visualize, we're giving our brains a blueprint of the person we want to become. We are experiencing what it feels like to act in a new way before it actually happens. This then makes it easier to play it out in real life because we've already been through the scenario in our minds and know what it feels like. This is how we deal with the weirdness of acting in a new confident way. This is how you can mentally prepare for parties, public speaking, or asking someone out because you've already been there in your mind and pictured it going well.

Visualization isn't some new age mumbo jumbo. There have been many scientific studies done on its positive effects. Dr. Maxwell Maltz stated that if your imagination is vivid and detailed enough, it tricks your nervous system into thinking it's actually real.[7] Like I mentioned earlier, I used to visualize myself as the confident person I wanted to become morning and night, and it became easier for me to act that way in public.

If you still need reassurance that this stuff actually works, check out some of the people who swear by it. Jim Carrey, Arnold Schwarzenegger, Oprah Winfrey and Will Smith just to name a few. There are many famous and successful athletes, entrepreneurs and entertainers who swear visualization mixed with action was the reason for their massive success.

# *Visualization Exercise*

So what I want you to do is take some time to think about the person you want to be.

*How do you act?*
*How do you think?*
*How do you talk?*
*How do you relate to others?*
*How are you in social settings?*
*What job do you do and how much money do you make?*
*What does your partner look like?*

## Step 1

Take out a pen and paper and describe the image you want to make in your mind in as much detail as you possibly can. It could be you giving a speech, asking your boss for a raise, or asking someone out. It could be the confident person you want to be or it could be all of the above. You can use this for anything you want to be *or* do.

Feel free to get creative here. Describe yourself as vividly and as real as possible. Pay attention to details, thoughts, sounds, smells, and feelings.

# Step 2

Once you've written down your ideal self or scenario (or both). Find a quiet place and take fifteen to twenty minutes a day to play your movie in your mind. Again, make it as real and vivid as you can. Really feel it in your body and become that confident version of yourself. Feeling is the most important thing here. Without feeling, it doesn't work as well.

*Note: This process is meant to be fun and feel good. Don't force it. If you're not enjoying it, you're not doing it right. If you're having trouble visualizing and getting a clear picture in your mind, try to imagine a movie character or someone whom you want to emulate and imagine how they would feel and act. Do your best without forcing it; each day, you'll get better and better at forming a clear picture in your mind. Don't give up; it's a very powerful technique.

# Step 3

Develop that image over time; work on it to make it better. Create other mind movies. You can use this technique for anything in your life you want to achieve, and, best of all, it's fun and feels good. Doing this exercise for twenty minutes each morning really worked for me, and I still do it to this day.

So have an open mind; give it a solid one to two-month trial, and I'm sure you'll begin to see results. This stuff really works; believe me!

*Reminder: Please, don't skip these exercises I'm giving you. Although they may seem like a lot of work, they're really important or I wouldn't have listed them. It doesn't matter if you think they're silly; just give them a try. Your current rituals obviously aren't working that well for you, so why not try something new? What have you got to lose?

## Further Reading

I got this exercise from a book (an audiobook) called *The New Psycho-Cybernetics* by Dr. Maxwell Maltz & Dan Kennedy. It's a real life changer and goes into much more detail about the powerful effects of a positive self-image and visualization.

# *I Remembered My Good Points and Wins*

Along with visualizing yourself as the confident person you want to be, take some time each day to remember all the things you like about yourself. I believe this is the most important thing you can ever do to grow your self-esteem, and I'll explain why.

What thoughts come to mind when I ask you to write down your positive qualities? Are you thinking something along the lines of *"there's nothing good about me"* or *"I have nothing worth writing down?"* Many people are quick to name all their flaws but have trouble thinking of their good points. They are constantly reinforcing all the things they dislike about themselves but very rarely reinforce any positives. This creates a negative spiral where the more you think of the bad things, the worse you feel about yourself and the more you begin to believe there is nothing good about you.

It isn't fair to only focus on the bad things while minimizing your good points; you would never do that to a friend, so why do you not deserve the same treatment? Everyone has things they're good at and can be proud of themselves for, but they very rarely acknowledge them or think they matter. They tell themselves their positive qualities don't count or are not important while their negative qualities matter a lot. But the truth is your positive qualities matter much more than your negative qualities. It's much harder to be a good person than to be a bad person. It's much harder to ask for help than to pretend everything is ok. It's much harder to work on yourself to improve your life than to stay in your comfort zone. It's much harder to listen than to talk.

It doesn't matter what they are or how small, just think of as many things as you can that you like about yourself and write them down. If you're having trouble with this exercise, as I did, let me give you a hand.

Do you always try to treat people with respect?

Do you look after your friends and family?

Have you ever given to charity?

What have you worked hard toward, achieved or know a lot about?

What skills and talents do you have?

What have others told you they like about you?

What qualities do you admire in others that you also possess?

What bad traits do you make an effort not to have?

What would your best friends or family say are your best traits?

How about this to start...

*Even though it's hard, I'm taking action to improve my life and overcome my social anxiety! I'm already doing better than 90 percent of others who don't take action to improve their lives.*

That's something to be proud of.

I must stress that you absolutely must stop minimizing your positive qualities if you ever hope to raise your self-esteem to a healthy level. It doesn't mean you need to be egotistical or tell everyone how good you are, but in your own head, you should always be reminding yourself what a good job you're doing. From now until eternity, treat yourself and speak to yourself like you would treat your closest friend or family member; that's how you should always look upon yourself and that's how I want you to complete this exercise.

Chances are, your relationship with yourself is severely damaged from years of self-rejecting behaviors and it's in desperate need of healing. Along with self-love and self-acceptance, this is another great way you can mend this relationship—by finally acknowledging your good points and giving yourself the credit you deserve.

Please, go ahead and do that now; list all the things you like about yourself and write them down, then reread them after you've finished your visualization exercise each day. This exercise is not a one off; this needs to be a daily practice, preferably twice daily. Spend a month doing this, once in the morning and once at night and keep adding to the list with things you did well the previous day. I'm sure it will raise your self-esteem to levels you never thought possible. This process really worked for me and I urge you to take it seriously.

# *I Stopped Comparing Myself to Others*

Society is always pitting us against each other. Every single day we hear things like:

*"He was top 1 percent in the country."*
*"He's the strongest."*
*"She's the fastest."*
*"My IQ is twenty points higher than average."*

*"She has a better body."*

Seriously, the list of ways we are compared to others could go on forever. It's in everything we do. We are taught from a young age to compare ourselves with everyone else to see where we fit in the social hierarchy. The trouble with comparing yourself to others is that it's like comparing apples to oranges. When you look at someone who is where you want to be or who you perceive to be better than you in some way, you get all down on yourself, and it's very harmful for your self-esteem.

The thing is, you haven't lived their life, and you haven't been through what they have. You're on your journey and they're on theirs. You don't know the kinds of experiences they've had, so you really can't compare. Everyone learns at their own pace and everyone is different. Just because someone is better than you at something—or taller, or prettier, or makes more money—doesn't make them any better a person than you.

When we look at others, we tend to only see their good points and pay less attention to their flaws. However, when we look at ourselves, we tend to focus more on our flaws and give little or no attention to our good points. It's not a fair fight, so to speak. We overestimate everyone else's skills and strengths and underestimate our own. This causes us to feel inferior and less capable around other people. You really need to watch this. Unfairly comparing yourself to other people is where an inferiority complex can begin.

Everyone has bad days. Everyone smells bad in the morning. Everyone says something stupid and makes mistakes now and again. Other people will be better than you at something, but you are better than them at something else. The key is to not let it faze you either way. We are all on different journeys and coming from different places.

When I was a young DJ, I used to compare myself to a famous DJ I wanted to be like. I would get down on myself because I wasn't as good as he was. But I failed to remember that he had been doing it for ten years and I had only been doing it for one year. It wasn't a fair comparison. If you want to have better social skills, don't compare yourself to a barman with ten years of experience talking to people for eight hours a night when you haven't been out for months. People do this kind of thing, then get down on themselves and say there's something wrong with them. No, he's just had ten more years of experience talking to people. That's all.

There's nothing wrong with looking up to others who are more successful and wanting to emulate their success, but you should only ever be comparing yourself with the person you were yesterday. Take yourself out of the race and any inferiority complex will begin to fade away. Doing this will help you become less anxious around others whom you perceive as better than you in some way.

## Key Points

1. Stop comparing yourself with others and only compete with yourself.
2. Everyone was born equal. Some have had more experience than others at certain things.

## *"Search Your Feelings, Luke."*

You need to become aware of when you're not feeling good, as this is a good sign there's something that needs to be dealt with. Our emotions tell us what is going on inside. If you can tune into how you're feeling more often, you'll notice when you're having a negative thought because you won't feel good. It might be bad self-talk, it might be picturing an event going poorly, or it could be feeling inferior to others.

The point is that your negative feelings are the signposts that something needs to be sorted out and healed. Paying attention to how I feel is my most effective method of catching my negative thoughts and challenging them. Before this, they slid past subconsciously and totally unchallenged.

## *I Chose My Company More Wisely*

I decided to stop hanging out and talking with people who didn't make me feel good about myself and found friends who did. This was INSTRUMENTAL in my healing.

I grew up in a rather toxic place—full of jealous, judgmental, and competitive people. I allowed other people to make me feel like I was inferior to them so they could feel better about themselves. Looking back now, the things they told me about myself didn't have anything to do with facts, but I believed these lies like they were the gospel truth, especially the one about me being "ugly."

Because I didn't really know who I was inside, I accepted other people's negative opinions of me as my own. It wasn't until I got out, saw the world, and met genuine people that I saw how toxic some of my old friends were for me. At the time, I didn't know any better; I thought it was normal for your friends to put you down. Finding a support network of people who allowed me to be myself without any judgment and who were supportive and encouraging toward me was a big turning point in my life.

Some friends, either consciously or subconsciously, try to put you down to make them feel better about themselves. Some friends get their validation by wanting to be the most confident, smart or funny person in your group. Some friends are cool as long as you're not doing better than them. As soon as you begin to improve yourself and get better results in your life, they change and become jealous. Some friends don't really want you to grow and become all you can be because then they'll feel bad about themselves; so, it's easier for them to pull you down rather than raise themselves up. A lot of old friends see you and treat you as you were, not how you are now or how you want to be. This also makes it hard to grow and change into someone new.

Another thing to look out for is this; when you start taking action to try and improve your life, some family members and friends may try to convince you that you're okay just the way you are. They may try to convince you that you don't need to change, even though you're not happy with your current circumstances. They mean well and they're not being bad people at all; just realize other people don't have to feel the pain of living *your* unfulfilled life.

If you want to find happiness, it's up to you to not allow anyone to knock you off course because if you do, you're the one who will pay for it, not them. Support from others is great but don't rely on it.

People grow, people change, and friends come and go. You're not obligated to remain friends with anyone who is continually putting you down and keeping you stuck. You need to take a look at each of your current friends, family, and role models and decide if these people are still right for you to spend time with. You don't owe anything to anyone who is making you feel badly about yourself, even if you've known them for a long time.

If you do have these types of people in your life, you should consider limiting the amount of time you spend with them. The famous motivational speaker Jim Rohn said that you're a mixture of the five people you hang out with the most. Be selective of whom you allow to influence you, especially when it comes to whose opinions you take on board. If others are constantly putting you down, making you feel worthless and not valued, are they really your friends anyway? Hang out with people on the same mission as you who will be supportive and nonjudgmental.

These people do exist and they're waiting to meet you. We invite you to come and join our private community of supportive and encouraging people all taking action to improve our lives at www.socialanxietyacademy.com.

While we're on the subject, you should also be aware of some of the people on the anxiety forums. I see many comments made by people who have obviously given up on themselves, have no motivation to overcome their anxiety and are looking for sympathizers. If you're not careful, they'll try to convince you that no one is capable of overcoming social anxiety, including you.

Don't allow anyone to tell you that you can't do something because they didn't do it. As always, use your own judgment and look for evidence of people who have done what you want to do rather than those who haven't.

## Key Points

1. You don't owe anything to anyone who is putting you down and making you feel bad about yourself.
2. Only spend time with people who make you feel good about yourself.

## *Give Thanks & Give to Others*

Many people today don't feel like they matter. They don't believe they're valuable or worth very much. If you're struggling with feelings of insignificance as I did for most of my life, as counterintuitive as it sounds, what helps me to feel valuable and wanted is to help and serve others.

When you help and serve others, whether through being a teacher, a mentor, a positive role model, a great friend, giving to charity, or helping those less fortunate than yourself, you will quickly realize you *do* matter and you are significant in people's lives. I believe we are all here to help each other. The more you give to others, the more you'll believe you are important and can make a positive difference in the world, and the better you will feel about yourself.

Sometimes we get so caught up in the drama of everyday life and all the things that aren't going well that we forget to appreciate what we do have. Each day, I try to take the time to think about things I'm grateful for...

*"I'm grateful for being healthy. I live in a safe country where I have the opportunity for an education. I can afford books and Internet to learn more about myself and the world. I have people in my life who love me and care about me and I have a roof over my head."*

When we give thanks and remember what we do have, it does two things. First, it rejuvenates your spirit and puts your troubles in perspective, and second, it attracts more good into your life because the universe responds to those who appreciate what they have and express gratitude for it.

## *EFT (Emotional Freedom Techniques)*

Something I've struggled with since I was a kid is replaying situations over and over again in my mind. I've had many sleepless nights, tossing and turning in my bed, continually replaying the day's events and what someone said or did to me. Anyone who can relate to this knows exactly how draining it can be. It's not like you want to keep replaying the scenario over and over again, but it just won't stop.

A great tool I've found for releasing all my forms of anxiety and obsessional thinking is EFT. You simply tap on certain meridian points of your body while thinking about something that gives you anxiety, and the negative feelings associated with the event dissolve.

EFT is now my go-to tool anytime I feel anxious or encounter a negative emotion that causes me pain. EFT works on many things including social anxiety, general anxiety, performance anxiety, OCD, dissolving the hurt from past traumas and upsetting events, clearing bad beliefs, fears, phobias, and physical pain. It's really quite amazing. I wouldn't believe it myself if I hadn't experienced the results first hand.

I have to admit I was pretty skeptical about it when my psychologist first asked me to try it with him. He told me it was a series of tapping movements on various acupressure points on the body. I thought it was weird and I couldn't see how tapping on parts of my body was going to help me forget past traumatic experiences or stop worrying about future ones. But I'm open to most things, so I gave it a try.

After we did two tapping rounds, which took about five minutes, I found myself unable to feel any negative emotion regarding the subject that we tapped about. I could remember the event clearly, but I couldn't feel bad about it anymore. I couldn't feel anything; it was neutral. I was totally blown away. My first thought was that it was the placebo effect and it would wear off after a while. But no, still to this day it works for me, so I will continue to use it.

It's a lifesaver when I'm about to walk into a social setting such as a party or nightclub and I'm feeling a little anxious. I just go to a quiet place like a bathroom stall and do my tapping. It really helped me through the initial stages of facing my social fears when my anxiety was still really high at parties, etc. I really want you to try this; I believe it could be life changing for you like it has been for me.

Here is another example of how EFT has helped me. I had been a bed-room DJ for many years, and it was always my dream to play in front of a big crowd. But I was always too nervous to ask club promoters if I could play in their club. I used EFT to bring down my anxiety and give me the confidence I needed to approach club promoters and ask them if I could do a gig. Eventually, after many rejections, I was awarded my first DJ gig, which, ironically, was playing the warmup set for a World's Top 10 DJ (to a full club of people). As you can imagine, I was the most nervous I've ever been—throwing up in the bathroom nervous. I used EFT tapping to bring my anxiety down to a manage-able level from a 10/10 to about a 4/10, and I could handle a four. If it weren't for tapping, I don't think I could've ever had that experience, so I'm very grateful I found it.

Along with using EFT to calm me down before a social event, I've used it to clear past traumatic experiences from my childhood that I was still holding onto. I let go of my fear of flying and let go of many of the negative beliefs I had about myself. The best thing is you don't even need to believe it's going to work for it to work. EFT is easy to learn and only takes around five to ten minutes to do; so, you have nothing to lose by giving it a try.

For further information, check out Gary Craig, the godfather of EFT. Other people who have taught me a lot about EFT are Carol Look and Nick Ortner.

Because EFT has helped me so much, in 2012 I became a certified EFT practitioner, so I can help others overcome their social anxiety. To find out more, please visit my website where I've created a course on how to use EFT specifically for social anxiety and clearing limiting beliefs. www.socialanxietyacademy.com

# What to Do When You're Feeling Anxious or Self-Conscious (This Is What I Did)

So far in the book, I've talked about a lot of mental concepts and things you can practice at home. You may now be wondering, "What happens when I'm in the middle of an anxiety attack or feeling very self-conscious in public? What tools did you use then?"

If I was ever feeling anxious or very self-conscious in public, here are some things I would do.

## EFT

If I were ever in the middle of an anxiety attack, feeling very fearful, or nervous that people were watching me, I found the nearest bathroom and did a tapping sequence. This would reduce my nerves considerably.

## See Yourself Through the Eyes of Other People

Another great strategy I picked up from CBT is to see myself through the eyes of other people when I felt self-conscious or was having an anxiety attack. I would ask myself:

*"If I saw someone else who looked nervous or self-conscious, would I judge them? Would I assume they're weak or stupid for being nervous? Would I laugh at someone who was having an anxiety attack or stuttered during a presentation? No, I wouldn't; so, that means others probably aren't laughing at me."*

## Stop, Breathe, and Repeat Mantra

When we get anxious, we forget to breathe, which only makes things worse. If I were ever feeling like everyone in the room was negatively judging me and I started to feel anxiety about it, I would focus on taking deep breaths and try to relax my body. Then I would stop what-ever I was doing and repeat this mantra:

*"What others think of me means nothing, and it's out of my control. I am who I am, no matter what they think. Let go."*

Our brains can only focus on one thing at a time, so focusing on breathing and repeating this mantra helps take away your focus on the fearful situation.

## Let Go and Accept without Fighting

I let go of trying to fight it and let it happen. I would remember no one really cares and no one is laughing at me; I was the only one who cared.

## I Remembered People Can't See How I Feel Inside

Sometimes, when we're anxious, we assume people can feel what we're feeling. But, in reality, people generally don't know how you feel inside and very rarely notice if you're anxious.

## Focus on Other People

Take the focus away from yourself and try to notice what other people are doing and saying. Our brains can only focus on one thing at a time, so focusing on others means you're not focusing on yourself.

Keep in mind these tools are helpful, but what's more important is to fix the causes, which are all the things we've discussed up until now plus the things we'll discuss in the remainder of this book. If you're trying to fix the symptoms once you're already having an anxiety attack or feeling self-conscious, it's too late. I feel this is where most people teaching this stuff are going wrong. They give you great advice for what to do when you're feeling anxious but fail to properly address the causes, therefore, the symptoms keep occurring. The way to fix the causes is to keep studying all the concepts discussed in this book and begin training your mind to think thoughts that are more helpful until it becomes second nature to you.

# *Irrational Fears*

To conclude the thoughts and beliefs section, I want to talk about fear. When you dig a little deeper, behind every kind of anxiety and feeling of inadequacy, lies fear. The common ones are:

*Fear of failure*
*Fear of judgment and criticism*
*Fear of rejection*
*Fear of abandonment*

I believe the reason most of us fear failure, judgment, criticism, rejection and abandonment so much is because they cause us great pain. We are biologically programmed to move away from pain, so it makes sense that in order to try and avoid pain, we form fears around anything that could potentially cause it.

I'm sure you will agree that emotional pain hurts far worse than physical pain and can last much longer. Broken bones can heal in weeks, whereas emotional pain and scarring can last a lifetime. That's why some daredevil stuntmen will have no problem surfing fifty foot waves but still have trouble approaching someone they find attractive. Emotional fear is the great equalizer and can bring three-hundred-pound men to their knees just as quickly as small children.

When you dig even deeper, eventually, you'll get to the mother of all fears.

# *Fear of Death*

There's a popular theory going around that suggests most of our social fears stem from the caveman days. Back then, if you were disliked and ostracized from the group, you faced death. If you were abandoned, you were out on your own with the animals. Death was a real possibility back then if people didn't like or approve of you, and you were rejected.

Unfortunately, our brains haven't updated to modern life. According to scientists, our brains are virtually the same as our ancestors' brains were thousands of years ago. What this means is we still have the same fears of abandonment that our ancestors had, but now days, these fears are totally irrational. In today's world, if someone rejects us, nothing happens. If someone doesn't like us, nothing happens. If we go to a party and no one wants to talk to us, nothing happens. If we ask someone on a date and they say no, nothing happens. We're totally safe.

Now days, there's absolutely no danger in social situations. We know this logically, but our brain is still wired to equate rejection, disapproval, criticism, and abandonment with the potential of death. Sure rejections and criticism don't feel nice at all, but surely, that's not enough to warrant such crippling anxiety. Of course, these fears are happening below the surface. We're not aware of why we feel socially nervous. We just get a strong feeling to freeze up, not to act, not to move, not to speak. This is our brain's way of keeping us safe from something it perceives to be a real threat to our survival because it's still operating on Windows 97 BC.

I'm telling you this to help you let go of judging yourself for feeling anxious. There's nothing wrong with you for feeling anxious or feeling some fear, especially when you're attempting to push outside of your comfort zone. When we do things we're not 100 percent comfortable with, like applying for a new job or talking to someone we deem to be important, anxiety and fear is a natural byproduct that occurs. Fear will never fully go away, but it does shows up less and less the more you do something and become comfortable with it.

Regardless of where our fears come from, they're still here and we still need to learn to deal with them effectively. It DOES NOT mean we should give in to the fears and let them rule our life. It's up to each of us to update our mind's OS (operating system) manually by using rational thinking. We need to continually remind ourselves that we're safe and there's no real danger in social situations anymore.

Are we able to overcome these irrational social fears? Absolutely. They do it with animals all the time. For example, horses are born with a fear of loud noises. This fear also stems back to the primitive days, where loud noises meant danger. If you try to ride an uninitiated horse near a highway with the roar of traffic, there's a good chance it could freak out and run right into oncoming traffic. This has actually happened many times.

So what they do is take the horse and tie it up next to the highway with loud trucks driving past. The horse freaks out for a while but then it learns that loud noises don't mean danger. After about a month or so, the fear of loud noises is gone and the horse can now walk on the road next to cars without freaking out.

The horse's brain has been rewired, and we can do the same with our fears.

For us humans, this is called exposure therapy. We need to slowly face the things that scare us and no longer run from them. After a short while, we see that there's no danger and socializing can, in fact, be safe and fun. The good thing is that we can do this gradually, starting really small and building up to more challenging tasks. This is what we'll be discussing in the next chapter.

# People Fear All the Wrong Things

You could say the types of fears I mentioned above are irrational fears—fears based on no real risk. However, as Tai Lopez suggests, there are some things in life we should actually fear that we don't.

For example:

*Why don't people fear wasting years or even decades of their lives being unhappy? Why don't they fear ending up alone or with someone they don't want to be with because they never sorted their confidence issues out? Or working a job they hate for forty years of their life because they feared to interview for a new job?*

Those are the real things to fear, not what other people think of your hair or the short-term pain and awkwardness of rejection. I wasted years of my life avoiding everything. I gave into my irrational fears and ended up lonely, working two minimum wage jobs, and depressed. I wasted my whole teens and twenties feeling empty and unhappy.

If you can learn to put your fears in perspective, it will help you overcome the irrational fears that are holding you back from happiness. Let the fear of long-term unhappiness inspire you to take action toward your dreams, even when you're feeling a little nervous. Time doesn't wait for anyone and you only get one life. Every day that passes you never get back. This isn't meant to make you feel bad, but that is the reality for all of us.

> *"And all that remained when his living was through was the mountain of things he intended to do tomorrow."* —John Canary

107

## *Easier Said than Done*

I understand most of the things we've discussed so far are much easier said than done. Believe me; I know. I've walked this path myself and had to overcome the seemingly unstoppable barrage of negative thoughts and emotions my mind was serving up on a daily basis.

Right now, these things we've discussed may seem impossible to stop. You need to give it time. As you become more aware, you'll realize when you're self-rejecting and acting in ways that are not in your best interests and then you'll be able choose a more helpful behavior.

You'll also be able to create a longer and longer gap between the thought itself and the physical manifestation of that thought (anxiety). Right now, it's happening so quickly it feels like they're one and the same, but actually, they're separate. The thought comes first, followed by the emotional and physical reaction in the body (fear and anxiety). With practice, you'll be able to separate the two and not allow yourself to be swept up by thoughts that cause fear and anxiety. You will be able to identify a negative thought and choose not to bite on it anymore.

Keep going and I promise you will see change soon enough!

## *Summary*

*"Mental strength is a lot like physical strength. If you want to be physically fit, you need to go to the gym, but to really get the best results, you need to give up eating junk food. Mental strength is the same. If you want to be mentally strong, you need to practice good mental habits, but you also need to give up your bad mental habits"* —Amy Morin

To end this chapter, I would like to go over a few of the main points. The process of overcoming social anxiety isn't an overnight thing; it takes time. Awareness is the first step to change, and I hope I've helped you become aware of some of the unhelpful mental habits that are contributing to your anxiety.

I recommend you read this chapter more than once. This isn't a book that you can read once and never read again. You need to train yourself to be continually aware of your negative thought patterns and choose thoughts that are more helpful. Some of the issues I highlighted have likely been going on for years and they won't be so easy to stop right away.

The most important thing is to accept where you currently are and stop judging yourself for it. If you're like me, you've been beating yourself up for way too long already. We're not going to do that anymore. From now on, we're going to stop handing our power over to everyone else by letting them control how we feel. We're going to let go of our need for other people to like us in order to like ourselves. We accept that judgment and criticism will happen no matter what, and we can't control it; so, it makes no sense to worry about it anymore.

I want you to realize you ALREADY ARE the person you want to be. Your reluctance to believe that fact is the only thing holding it back from you. There's nothing you have to go out and get or do. This whole process of healing social anxiety is more about unlearning and stopping behaviors, rather than having to learn how to become someone different.

Now that we're armed with these new mental tools, they'll act like a mental suit of armor when we go out and grow our social confidence. This leads us into the next chapter about taking action.

## 2

# ACTIONS & EXPOSURE

## *Facing Your Social Fears*

**T**HIS IS THE PART where a lot of people begin to get nervous. Building my social confidence was the part that brought me the most anxiety in the beginning, and you're probably feeling the same.

Don't worry, it's not going to be as hard or scary as you may think. Depending on where you currently are, you may only need to change the way you view your everyday social interactions. Let me explain…

Now that you're equipped with your new mental tools, instead of looking at social situations as a burden, hard word, or scary, begin viewing the everyday social situations you find yourself in as practice. Every social interaction you encounter throughout your day is another chance for you to practice your new skills.

That's the mindset that helped me through this process. Every conversation and social setting was another opportunity for me to improve my skills and measure how much progress I'd made; so I tried to get myself in as many as possible. Because I viewed it as a game and a new skill I was learning, it helped me not take it personally if a conversation got awkward or I got nervous. After each interaction, I picked out what I did right and what I'd like to improve for the next time. Treating it like a skill I was learning helped separate me from my results.

A 9 week social exposure plan will help to supercharge your results (I will talk about that later in the book), but it's not essential as long as you place yourself into plenty of social situations each day and try not to avoid them. Of course, if you're totally avoiding any form of social situation throughout your day, then you will need to slowly begin facing them if you hope to overcome social anxiety. The key is to *slowly* confront our social fears on a more regular basis and build up momentum as we get more comfortable.

## *Introversion Isn't a Weakness*

Many people think being introverted is the same thing as being shy. What I've come to understand is introversion and shyness are two different things and there are many people in the world who are introverted but not shy. In fact, some of the world's most successful inventors, musicians, speakers, and artists are introverts.

The difference between an introvert and an extrovert is where they draw energy from. Extroverts gain energy from being with people. They thrive on social situations and group settings. They like to work in teams, speak up, and share their ideas.

Introverts draw energy from alone time. They enjoy spending time alone and need quiet time to think and reflect. Social situations can often drain introverts; they need to balance socialising with equal amounts of alone time so they can recharge their batteries.

While it is common that introverts are also shy, being introverted does not necessarily mean you *are* shy. I consider myself a very introverted person, but I am no longer shy. I now enjoy and feel comfortable socialising, but I also need my alone time to feel replenished. If you consider yourself to be an introvert, it's important to understand this distinction; realize there's nothing wrong with you for wanting to spend time alone to recharge.

Becoming more social and overcoming social anxiety as an introvert can get tricky. Introverts like to be alone, but it should never be used as an excuse to be a hermit. Socialising and relationships are an important part of life, and important for physical health too. A study done in the journal *Perspectives on Psychological Science March 2015 10: 227-237* found that social isolation (or lacking social connection), and living alone were found to increase mortality rates by around 30%.

Don't freak out if you are someone who spends most of your time alone, but realize it's important to have a balanced life. The key is finding a healthy balance between being alone and socialising. As an introvert, I've found socialising too much can leave me feeling drained; that's why I've suggested throughout this book the 50/50 rule. Spend half your free time socialising and the other half alone. That's what seems to work best for me.

## Further Reading

*Quiet: The Power of Introverts in a World That Can't Stop Talking* by Susan Cain

# *Fear of Failure: Processing Failure and Rejection the Right Way*

When I'd go out at night to face my social fears and build my confidence, I made an effort to learn from people who seemed to be really socially comfortable. For example, I'd watch men walk up to women to start a conversation. Some men would get rejected and go scurrying back to their corner and not speak to anyone for the rest of the night (that was me). However, other men would go from woman to woman, sometimes, getting totally blown out but never letting a rejection even faze them.

I had to learn more. I was shocked by how someone could be that mentally bulletproof to get totally rejected and not even blink or let it affect their mood at all. I also studied people in business, the kind of people who could walk into the dragon's den or shark tank and pitch their life's work, only to have it totally shot down and told it was worthless on national TV, yet walk out still smiling and positive. I'd have been in tears!

What I've noticed is that confident people perceive failure differently than insecure people. Confident people see failure as simply feedback. They don't take failure or rejection personally; they see it as a stepping stone. They take what's not working, then correct course and move forward. Insecure people take failure or rejection personally. They take rejections to heart. The danger with taking failure personally is:

*"I failed at x"* can quickly turn into *"I'm a failure at everything."*

But here's the thing… **you're not your results.** You're not your looks. You're not your bank account, your job, or your thoughts. Truly secure people know that. They've learned to separate themselves from their results. They fail and they keep trying; their identity isn't attached to their results, job, or looks. They don't get their validation (good feelings) from external sources; they get it from within themselves, from having the guts to face their fears and go after what they desire. This means that when they get rejected or told no, it doesn't bother them all that much.

You need to learn (as I did) to separate yourself and your identity from your results. You're not a failure because you failed at something and you're not worthless because someone rejected you.

> *"Your value doesn't decrease based on someone's inability to see your worth." —Anonymous*

Once you get this—I mean really internalize it and not take failure or rejection personally—you'll be well on your way to building rock-solid social confidence.

## *Things Will Be Different Now (You Have the Mental Tools)*

All of the mental concepts I've shared with you thus far are critical in helping you overcome social anxiety and keeping you from giving up when it gets hard. I feel the main reason people don't see results when trying to overcome social anxiety is they don't have the mental tools to effectively deal with the situations that cause them discomfort.

*But now that you do, things will be different!*

Remember; the past does not equal the future unless you still live there. With each day and each new situation, we learn, grow, and become better. If you've tried to overcome social anxiety in the past and didn't get the outcome you wanted, I want you to give it another go. Now, when you go out and take action, you know not to take an awkward conversation personally. Now, you reward yourself for having the guts to try instead of only rewarding yourself for a positive outcome. Now, you're aware that some people will always judge, and you don't pay any attention to what people think of you. Now, you know how to visualize to change your self-image and to only focus on your good points and things you did well. Finally, now you know not to pay attention to that critical voice in your head telling you why you aren't capable.

Once we put less importance on what others are thinking of us, stop being our own worst critic, and, instead, choose to accept ourselves and be our own best friend, the pressure gets lifted and we begin to feel more comfortable around people. This makes growing our social confidence much easier and more fun. This won't happen overnight, but give it time. It will happen; I assure you. I'm living proof of that.

# *You Need to Have a Strong Reason WHY*

It's hard to get motivated to take action when you don't have a strong enough reason why. Thinking about and writing down all the positive ways your life will change makes it easier to get the motivation to do what you need to do. You need to get emotionally involved with this process. When you do, you'll be able to move mountains in your life.

## Why Do You Want to Overcome Social Anxiety?

How will your life change once you get this area handled?

How will your dating and romance life improve?

What kind of job will you have?

How will your social life look?

How will you feel when you're more confident?

116

Write your answers to the above questions on your phone and read them often. You need to keep the benefits of taking action to overcome social anxiety firmly fixed in your mind. Believe me, all this effort will be worth it when you're kissing your special someone for the first time or walking through the world with confidence (or whatever goal it may be for you).

So go ahead and make that list now. Make a list of the short-term and long-term reasons why you want to achieve this goal and keep them in mind as you read through this chapter.

## *Confidence Comes from Practice*

To gain true confidence in anything, we must do it repeatedly. For example, if you want to become confident talking to someone you find attractive (which is a big one for most people), you need to get out there and start practicing. As they say, *"competence builds confidence."*

We need to start creating new positive reference experiences that challenge our old limiting beliefs. Positive reference experiences are so important because they provide real-life proof. Remember what we talked about in the beliefs section and exercises? Positive social experiences really help these new positive beliefs sink in and become fact for you. For example, it becomes really hard to keep believing you're shy if you've been out socializing four times this week, had fun, and made a lot of new friends.

This is how you build social confidence—one experience at a time, one day at a time. The more positive reference experiences you can give yourself, the more confident you'll become in a shorter amount of time. This is how I did it. I created new positive experiences that challenged the negative beliefs I had about myself. I had a belief for my whole life that I was shy and not a people person. This belief was never challenged because I was continually avoiding socializing. So, as I mentioned earlier, I first got rid of the label: "I'm shy," and, instead, I told myself, "I've been electing shy behaviors all my life, but today, I choose to try something different."

Then I made myself go out and socialize, even if I didn't feel like it. It was so much easier for me to feel comfortable in social situations once I let go of the outcome, the fear of judgment, and the need to be perfect.

Over the course of the next few months, I had many great experiences and a few awkward ones too. I made new friends and I was going on some dates. I saw I could do well in social situations. I found socializing could be fun and, most importantly, *I noticed there were times when I wasn't feeling anxious.*

I used these new positive experiences as a reference to challenge my old beliefs. I asked myself things like:

*"How is it possible that I was born shy if I wasn't shy tonight?"*

*"How can I have social anxiety for life and a chemical imbalance in my brain when I didn't feel anxiety for most of tonight?"*

With all these new positive experiences, my beliefs about myself began to change. I don't think many of us realize what we're really capable of. Most of us think of ourselves as average and not capable of doing the things that other people can do; so, we don't even try. But we're all capable of greatness and certainly all capable of being comfortable in social interactions. Not until we get out there and really try will we realize what we're truly capable of and how good we could actually be.

One thing I want to make clear is there will always be a little bit of fear during this process, especially in the beginning. Everyone in the world feels fear when they do things they are not comfortable with. This process is not about getting rid of feeling fear; it's about feeling fear and doing it anyway, because we understand it's for the betterment of our lives. Yes, in the short term, your anxiety may rise a bit, but facing your social fears will massively reduce your anxiety long term.

Once I made the commitment to no longer avoid social situations, mixed with accepting myself even with all my flaws and then changing my negative self-talk, my seemingly indestructible wall of social anxiety began crumbling in a short time—only a few months in fact. Just like in *The Wizard of Oz*, I peeked behind the curtain of my fears to see a tiny little man pulling the strings. I realized my fears were all illusory.

> *"Fear is not real. The only place fear can exist is in our thoughts of the future. It is a product of our imagination, causing us to fear things that do not at present, and may not ever exist. That is near insanity. Do not misunderstand me, danger is very real, but fear is a choice."* —Will Smith

## There Will Always Be Pain

Our whole lives, we try to run away from pain. It's one of our two fundamental survival principles—to move away from pain and toward pleasure. In my experience, moving away from pain is a much more powerful driver than taking action toward long term pleasure. That's why many people waste years of their lives stuck in jobs and relationships they don't like but never do anything to change it. They are comfortable where they are, even if they're not happy. The anticipated pain of having to take action is greater than the pleasure they think they would get from the change, so they don't do anything.

119

We're all guilty of it. We avoid the things that make us nervous and end up settling nice and safe in our comfort zones. The thing is, it's not really all that comfortable, is it?

*Are you truly happy or just comfortably avoiding pain?*
*Do you feel good about yourself and your current social life?*
*How about your career and love life?*

If you've read this far, you probably have some sort of pain you're trying to heal. Perhaps it's loneliness, isolation, self-doubt, low self-esteem, or you're not where you want to be in your career, and money is tight.

I have found that it's much harder to motivate ourselves to take action when the pain is sharp and intense—like the uncomfortable feeling you get before you go to your first dancing class and you don't know anyone, or the panic you feel when thinking about asking someone out on a date or applying for a new job. This kind of pain is intense, but for a much shorter period. Even though we know doing these things will make our lives better long term, it's still hard to get ourselves to actually do it.

So instead, we avoid it. We decide to stay at home by ourselves on the weekend—dreaming of having someone to spend our lives with, feeling bored and lonely, dreading Monday where we will have to go back to the job we hate. This is also pain, but it's just not as intense in the short term and you can take your mind off it with alcohol, drugs, overworking, or the vice of your choice. However, the pain of living an unfulfilled life is a much worse pain. It's a long, drawn-out, depressive type of pain. The kind of pain that makes you feel empty and like there's something missing.

*"We must all suffer from one of two pains: the pain of discipline or the pain of regret. The difference is, discipline weighs ounces while regret weighs tons."* —Jim Rohn

Which would you rather carry around for the rest of your life?

So, now that we've established there will be pain no matter what we do, what kind will you choose? The short-term uncomfortable feeling of taking action to change your life and then enjoying the long-term happiness it brings? Or the long, drawn-out, depressive pain of staying where you currently are?

# *The Uncomfortable Comfort Zone*

If you want to achieve your goals in life, if you want to attract your dream lover or your dream job, even if you just want to become more confident, sooner or later, you're going to have to get out of your comfort zone. You're going to have to leave your safe zone and put yourself in situations where you can grow, learn, and potentially be criticized, rejected or told no. In order to get the life of your dreams, you're going to have to become comfortable with sometimes being uncomfortable.

One of my favorite quotes from Robert Allen who co-wrote the book *The One Minute Millionaire* is:

*"Everything you want is just outside your comfort zone."*

I can definitely relate to that. To achieve everything good in my life, I had to get out of my comfort zone. It sucked, I didn't want to do it, I was scared and I complained. But I did it anyway because I knew it was better than the other option, which was for things to stay the same as they were and continue to be broke, miserable and alone.

I'm sorry, but there's no way around it. If you want more in your life than you have right now, you're going to have to get out of your comfort zone. But what you may not realize right now is that getting out of your comfort zone is when the real magic and growth happens in your life. Yes, it can be uncomfortable at times, but the pain that comes from not having confidence is far worse than the small pain it takes to build it.

Think of getting out of your comfort zone like getting into a cold shower. You really don't want to get in, you delay it, you procrastinate, but then you finally take the plunge. Once the water hits your skin, it stings for a few seconds, but then what happens? You get used to it after a short while. How do you usually feel after taking a cold shower? More awake and refreshed, right?

It's exactly the same in life.

Getting out of your comfort zone will sting a bit at the start, but you'll feel much better afterward. Not only that, but your comfort zone will expand. So the next time you go to do it, it will be easier for you and feel less uncomfortable. It becomes a snowball effect where you keep gaining momentum with every new thing you do. The more you get out of the comfort zone, the more you grow and the better your quality of life becomes. Getting out of your comfort zone also builds healthy self-esteem because we like ourselves more when we take action, show courage, and go for what we want in life.

## How Much Do You Want to Change Your Life?

If you'd rather sit at home and make excuses as to why you can't do it, complain, and blame someone else, then nothing anyone says or does is going to help you.

The world is full of people like that.

122

But I don't believe you're that type of person. The fact that you've read this far tells me you want out of your current circumstances.

Well, you're almost there.

I've led you to the precipice, but I can't make you take the plunge. Only you can do that. I've given you everything you need except for one thing; the final thing you'll need is some good old-fashioned courage.

# *Courage: The #1 Confidence Builder*

Courage is saying to yourself:

*"You know what, I'm feeling nervous about this and I don't know what the outcome is going to be, but I'm going to do it anyway because I know it's the right thing to do for my future happiness."*

For every ounce of courage you can muster, you'll be rewarded in equal amounts with confidence; I guarantee you that. The more out of your comfort zone you can go, the more confident you'll become.

Heroes aren't the only ones with courage, everyone has courage inside of them, some just don't use it very often. Courage is also like a muscle; the more you use it and practice it, the stronger it becomes. Showing courage also builds self-esteem because when we face a fear and do something that intimidates us, we feel really proud of ourselves. It will take a little bit of courage to begin doing things you're not used to doing; but I assure you, it will be worth it when you experience how good you feel afterward.

> *"Do the thing you fear the most and the death of that fear is certain."* —Ralph Waldo Emerson

123

# *Rationalizations & Excuses: Are You Lying to Yourself to Justify Your Avoidance Behaviors?*

In my experience, there are two main reasons people don't get everything they want in life. The first is lack of awareness; they don't know what they're doing wrong or what needs to be changed in order to get to where they want to be. The second is what I want to talk about now. Rationalizations. They know what they have to do but make excuses to justify why they can't.

**Rationalization** Verb – To ascribe (one's acts, opinions, etc.) to causes that superficially seem reasonable and valid but are actually unrelated to the true, possibly unconscious and often less credible or agreeable causes.

**Rationalization** Noun – (psychiatry) A defense mechanism by which your true motivation is concealed by explaining your actions and feelings in a way that's not threatening.

When going through this whole process, it's important to remember that your brain will always be trying to trick you into staying in your comfort zone where it's safe. But we both know where that road leads. Sometimes, the *real* reasons for why you don't want to act will be hidden, and, instead, your brain will give you a convenient excuse. For example, you may be procrastinating about going to a party and having to socialize.

You might be telling yourself, "I'm tired," or, "I have too much work to do tomorrow."

But the real reason is:

"I feel nervous about going to this party because I'll have to talk to people I don't know."

## Are You Lying to Yourself?

You may find yourself making all kinds of rationalizations and excuses for not taking action to overcome your social anxiety. Be aware when you start to say things to yourself like:

*"I don't need to be socially confident. It won't help me. My life is not that bad and I enjoy being single. People are weird anyway; I prefer to be by myself."*

Do you really truly mean that? Or is it just an excuse to not have to act and get out of your comfort zone? You may also be looking for any excuse to dismiss this information. You may tell yourself something like:

*"I already tried this and it doesn't work for me. I don't respond well to facing my social fears. Medication is the only thing that works for me."*
*"I wouldn't be seen dead in a bar or club. Clubs are for pretentious snobs."*
*"This guy is just another snake oil salesman trying to sell me something."*
*"Just because it worked for him doesn't mean it will work for me. He doesn't know me or what I've been through. I'm different."*
*"I don't have time to try all these things. I'm too busy."*
*"This only applies to an x type person, and I'm a y type person."*

Again, no judgment here, but you *really* have to watch those justifications and rationalizations; they're the very things that keep us stuck for so long. Search your true motivations behind those kinds of comments if you have them. Also try to identify any other excuses you may be telling yourself that are holding you back.

I'm not saying the above statements are necessarily wrong. Maybe you really do believe some of the excuses you tell yourself. What's important is not whether you believe them, but whether they are going to get you where you want to go in life.

*Do you want to make excuses or get results? You can't have both!*

Again, I'm only writing this because I used to do all of this myself. It doesn't feel nice when someone challenges our long-held belief systems or tells us it's nobody else's fault but our own. It's the equivalent of someone coming in to wake us up at 5 a.m. on a cold winter's morning. Our first reaction is to lash out at the person, tell them to go away, and crawl back into our comfort zone under the covers. What we're really doing when we rationalize is lying to ourselves in order to make us feel better for not doing the things we know we need to do.

# *I Stopped Making Excuses*

I used to make all kinds of excuses to get out of taking action. Here are some lines my mind would throw at me. Do any of these sound familiar?

*"I'm too tired."*
*"I don't feel like it today."*
*"I'll do it tomorrow."*
*"I have too much work to do."*
*"I need to save my money, so I can't go out."*
*"I have to get up early tomorrow."*
*"I'm definitely starting this diet/gym/taking action on Monday."*
*"I don't do small talk."* (I loved that one.)
*"She doesn't look friendly."*
*"She's probably in a relationship."*
*"I'm not good looking enough to speak to her."*
*"There's no use even trying; I was born this way."*

*"I don't know how to dance."*
*"I have no one to go out with tonight."*
*"I don't know anyone at the party, so I can't go."*

Then they started getting ridiculous...

*"My clothes are wrinkled and my iron isn't working; I don't want to be seen in wrinkled clothes, so I can't go out tonight."*
*"My car's on empty. I'd have to go to the gas station and fill up; it's just too much hassle."*

Think about some of the excuses you may have been using and ask yourself:

*Are they serving you or holding you back?*

Some of your excuses are probably valid; maybe you do have to wake up early or you do feel tired. But no excuse is acceptable if you want to see real change in your life. When you commit to something, you have to fully commit. When you give in to your excuses, you give yourself a way out, and your brain is always looking for a way out. All it takes is to give in to your excuses just once and the next time you plan to go out, your brain will think:

*All I have to do is make us feel tired, and then we won't have to do this thing we really don't want to do.*

Every time we give in to our excuses, it becomes harder to do things the next time. When I was first starting to become more sociable, I used to conveniently get *really tired* just before I had to go to a party, even if I hadn't done anything that day to make me feel tired. I knew it was my brain trying to trick me into staying in and watching a movie instead of going out and socializing, and with that awareness, I wasn't going to let that happen.

Once you train yourself that rain, hail or shine, you're going to that dancing class/disco/party/book club, regardless of what excuse your brain is throwing at you, your brain falls into line really quickly and, all of sudden, you get a boost of energy. I know this from experience. I also know that even though it can be hard to motivate yourself to go, you ALWAYS feel better about yourself afterward, and 99 percent of the time, you end up enjoying it.

## I Held Myself Accountable

This is probably the thing I struggle with most in life, holding myself accountable for following through on the things I know I need to do. In the beginning, there may be times when you want to give up, stop, or have a week off. Next thing you know, you haven't left the house for months, and you're right back at the start again.

You have to remind yourself constantly of why you're making this effort. We talked previously about having a strong WHY, and I got you to write down all the reasons why you want to change your life and all the benefits that will come. This next exercise is the opposite of that.

## Deathbed Exercise

Another exercise that helped me was to think about what life would be like for me if I DIDN'T change. How will my life be in twenty years' time if I continue down the same path of avoidance behaviors? I used to picture myself on my deathbed thinking about all the things I would regret. All of a sudden, I had the leverage I needed to be sociable, even when I didn't feel like it. Remembering some of the things that you're not happy about in your life can be a great tool for motivation, as long as you don't dwell on them or judge yourself for them. Just use them for motivation to take action.

What I want you to do now is take out the list of WHYS you wrote earlier and underneath it, write a few sentences about what you'll regret if you were on your deathbed. This is an extremely powerful motivational tool for change.

# *Conversation Techniques & Social Skills*

Developing social skills and conversation techniques is a big topic and whole books have been written on this subject alone. In this book, I just want to share with you some quick-start tips to get you up and running ASAP. It helps to feel more comfortable starting conversations when you have a few conversation techniques up your sleeve.

Many people are afraid of the awkward silence in conversations and running out of things to say, so they shy away from initiating conversations with people they'd like to know better.

## Tip 1 — Icebreaker: Give a Compliment

If you want to start a conversation with someone but don't know what to say, you can never go wrong with a compliment. Genuine compliments always go down well and almost never fail. Tell someone you like their shoes or belt, then ask where they got it.

Then you can follow up with something like, "What are your plans for the weekend?" The person will answer and usually ask you the same question back. To this, you reply what your plans are for the weekend, and away you go.

## Tip 2 — AWKWARD SILENCE TIP! Ask Questions

129

If you ever find yourself caught in the middle of an awkward silence, follow this simple tip: *Ask a question.*

Have a couple of go-to questions you've memorized beforehand. They can be anything at all such as, "Do you know any good restaurants around here? I'm looking to try something new." Or, "Where's the best place you've ever visited? I'm planning my next vacation and looking for ideas."

It doesn't really matter what the question is; people love talking about themselves and their lives. Have a few prepared because, when you're in the middle of an awkward silence, you may freeze up if you have to think on the fly. If you have a general script prepared, it will give you more confidence to start conversations with people, and you won't be so concerned about running out of things to say.

Once they reply to your question, relate it back to your own life and experiences. For example, if they say they went to Brazil, you can say, "Oh cool, I met a Brazilian once; he was nice. I'd like to go there," etc. Keep asking questions and then making statements related to what they said. This is all that's involved in a good conversation.

Don't worry about the conversation appearing boring or not witty enough. Conversations don't always have to be about the theory of relativity; most conversations are about normal everyday subjects. People won't be judging you on your originality.

Remember to try and maintain eye contact with the person, especially when you're talking. It doesn't have to be the whole time, but do try your best to look at people's faces when you talk to them.

Finally, accept that awkward silences happen; they're normal, and it's not always your fault. There are two or more people in a conversation, and it's up to everyone to contribute, not just you. Remember, people will still like you and a conversation can still be great even if there are a few silences in between. You don't always need to be talking for someone to enjoy your company.

# Tip 3 — Be present and Interested in What They're Saying

It's hard to focus on two things at once. The more you focus on the other person and what they're saying, the less you focus on yourself and how nervous you feel. A good technique I've found is to listen to them as if you were going to be quizzed on what they said afterward. If you *really* listen to what they're saying, you won't have time to notice you're feeling anxious, and you won't get stuck in your own head. Plus, the other person will appreciate you being interested in what they're saying and you may form a new friendship.

# More Tips

1.  Try to get out of your own head as much as possible and be curious about the other person; pay more attention to what other people are doing and less about how you're coming across.

2.  It's okay to show a little vulnerability. You can admit to people that parties make you a little nervous or that you never know what to say to break the ice. People won't judge you for being honest; they'll appreciate it, and it will allow them to relax more too.

3.  Talk about what you like. Start sentences with: "I love it when…." or, "You know what I really like…."

4.  When conversations end, don't take it personally. All conversations end. If you need to end it, politely excuse yourself and say it was nice to meet them.

# *Social Confidence Building Exercises: Some of the Ways I Became More Social*

## I Made the Effort to Talk to Everyone I Met

Barristers, bartenders, taxi drivers, waiters, shopkeepers; I made an effort to speak to everyone I encountered during my day. I realized that people actually are friendly and nice and it's totally normal to talk with strangers. Some people have been conditioned since childhood to "never talk to strangers." That may have been sound advice for children, but not for adults. Just as we learned to cross the street without holding someone's hand, we can learn to size up strangers so we can feel safe talking with them. At the start I had to force myself to do it, but the more I made small talk with people and got to know them, the better I became at it and the more comfortable I felt. I also made a lot of new friends and found out all kinds of new and interesting information. It's surprising the things you can learn just by being friendly and talking to everyone.

## I Got off My Phone and Became Present

Go to any restaurant these days and you'll see most people on their mobile phones. Couples, families, and friends out for a nice dinner together and instead of being present and enjoying each other's company, they have their heads down checking their Facebook and Instagram, completely ignoring one another.

This has become an epidemic, and it's only getting worse. We spend all day on the computer and our phones not talking to anyone face to face. Then we wonder why we lack social skills and feel uncomfortable around people. People have forgotten to be present and effectively communicate with each other. I have family members and friends who are just never present when they're with me. Most of the time, they aren't even listening to what I'm saying. They're more concerned with their virtual friends than the one in real life sitting in front of them.

I made a rule to get off my phone when I'm out with people and talk, connect, and be present. Some groups have a rule when they go out to all put their phones in the middle of the table and the first one to touch it has to pay for the dinner. That's a good way to break the habit of checking your phone every two minutes when you're out with people.

## Assertiveness — I Stopped Letting Things Slide

In the past, I would always let things slide. If someone cut in front of me in line, I wouldn't speak up about it. I would let it slide and justify my passiveness by telling myself, *"It doesn't matter; we're all going to get served eventually."*

But deep down, I was angry at that person for cutting in front of me and angry at myself for not saying anything. I realized this avoidance behavior wasn't helping me. I made a commitment to myself that if there ever was a time I wanted to speak up about something, I had to speak.

Letting things slide and not speaking up for yourself when someone violates your boundaries is really harmful to your self-esteem and perhaps even your physical health too.

Maybe someone isn't cleaning up after themselves at home, but you don't say anything. Maybe someone is having double standards with you; it's okay for them but not for you. Maybe someone is always late to your meetings and not valuing your time. There could be any number of things. The way to know is to ask yourself:

*"Is this person's actions making me feel angry/upset/annoyed/devalued, etc.?"*

133

If the answer is yes and you're not speaking up about it, then you must start today. Each time you don't stand up for yourself, each time you let things slide, you lose a little more respect for yourself. Wouldn't you agree it's far better to sort the problem out as it arises and then get on with your day than it is to hold onto anger and resentment for weeks and sometimes even years? A lot of the time, the person doesn't even realize you don't like the way they're acting until you tell them.

Being assertive doesn't mean going out and starting arguments, fights, yelling at people, and calling them abusive names. It simply means, when someone is violating your boundaries, when someone is making you feel annoyed or devalued, you simply politely tell them how it's making you feel and you wish them to stop.

Being polite doesn't mean being a pushover or asking in an approval-seeking manner such as, *"I was wondering, if it's not too much trouble, if you could maybe stop doing that thing. It's okay if you don't want to, though."* Being assertive and polite means asking in a firm, calm, but diplomatic way so that you can achieve a win-win situation. You can achieve your goals of being happy and not being annoyed while also not making the other person feel attacked or resentful.

Whenever we run from confrontation, it gets harder to be assertive the next time; but each time we face it, it becomes easier and our confidence in ourselves grows. You owe it to yourself to begin to stick up for yourself; you deserve to be happy and you shouldn't ever put up with poor treatment.

## I Made Socializing a Priority

No more spending my whole weekend at home on the computer or reading a book. I allowed myself to read or be alone 50 percent of my free time. The other 50 percent I spent socializing. I went to bars, clubs, house parties, self-improvement programs, dancing classes, you name it.

## I Had More Fun and Stopped Taking Life So Seriously

Overcoming social anxiety is all about building self-acceptance, self-esteem, thinking more helpful thoughts, and letting things go. A good way to build a habit of self-love and letting things go is to try to have more fun in your life. Sometimes, I get so caught up in always striving to be better that I forget to stop and smell the roses. I've since made an effort to do more things that bring me joy, such as surfing, hanging out with my friends, and watching sunsets. Spending time outside in the sun has been shown to increase serotonin, the feel-good hormone, and is used in treating seasonal depression.

Give yourself permission to be less serious and do more of what makes you happy and brings you joy. Learning to become more confident can be fun! There is just as much joy to be found in the journey and the person you become along the way as there is in reaching the destination.

## Further Reading

There's a book about this very subject called *Play It Away* by Charlie Hoehn. The author describes how he cured his general anxiety and panic attacks through having more fun, living a healthy lifestyle and working less. It's a great read.

## I Stopped Relying on Alcohol As a Crutch

I had always relied on getting completely wasted drunk before I had the confidence to talk to anyone. The thing about drinking is that it doesn't give you real long-term confidence. It's fake confidence that disappears by the morning. So I gave myself a two-drink rule. I wasn't allowed any more than two drinks the whole night. Socializing while sober is where the real growth comes from.

Binge drinking all the time was making my general anxiety and depression worse, so cutting it out helped me four-fold. My health improved along with my confidence. I saved lots of money, and I felt great the next day, too. I still don't binge drink today because I realized I don't need it and I never needed it.

*Note: This is an optional exercise.* If you have to choose between drinking at a party to calm your nerves or staying at home, I would choose to drink because at least you're still out being sociable. But when you no longer need it as a crutch, try putting it aside and see how you feel.

## I Took Confidence-Building Programs to Become a Better Person

If you don't feel like you have good social skills with people, there's nothing wrong with getting a little help. It's no different from getting help with your golf swing or your math, in my opinion. We all have our strengths and weaknesses. Some people are naturally good talkers and some are more introverted, but we can all learn to become good at anything we put our minds to.

If getting help makes you feel more confident and makes it easier for you to leave the house and meet people, then I'm all for it. To gain a lot of confidence in a short amount of time, I would highly recommend looking into taking a dating boot camp or joining toastmasters (www.toastmasters.org). Toastmasters is a club that holds regular meetings for people who want to learn how to feel more comfortable with public speaking. They're very supportive and understanding and there's never any judgment. The group is mostly made up of people who have a fear of public speaking and/or want to improve their public speaking skills. Toastmasters is great if you want to gain social confidence in a very short time. When you do these kinds of confidence building activities, you'll be able to see the change taking place in you right before your eyes.

## I Joined a Yoga Class

I was nervous and intimidated at the start and didn't want to go. I didn't want to look like a fool in front of everyone. The people in my yoga school ended up being really friendly. No one cared about what I looked like or how good I was. (I was the only one worrying about that.)

Most of them just wanted to help me and get to know me. I've made quite a few good friends from my yoga class that I still hang out with today. I would highly recommend yoga to anyone with anxiety or depression. Not only do you get the benefit of meeting new people but you also improve your health, flexibility, thinking, breathing, and you become a more centered person.

## *Designing Your Own Social Exposure Plan*

Designing your own social exposure plan is a complicated and delicate subject, and I could write a whole book on this alone. This is one of, if not *the* most, important and critical parts of your success, and I encourage you to please take this process seriously. This has to be something you put some time and thought into. The exposures have to be enough to get you out of your comfort zone and grow your confidence while not so daunting that you'll be overwhelmed and give up or, even worse, not even start. You will also benefit from having someone there to make sure you follow through. As someone who has gone through this process three times, I can tell you that having the support of a community or friends makes it a hundred times easier to follow through and succeed.

*If you would like some help with this process, I encourage you to check out my nine-week online program. I've designed the course to help you ease into taking the first few steps of your social exposure plan and not get too overwhelmed.*

*The best part is you'll have (optional) access to a community of like-minded non-judgmental people all taking part and you can post your progress in the group chat for encouragement. I will also be there to guide you through the process, answer questions and provide support along the way. For more information, please visit* www.socialanxietyacademy.com.

# Steps to Designing Your Own Exposure Action Plan

# Step 1 — Make a List from Least to Worst

Start by making a list of the social experiences you would like to be able to do that scare you the least, all the way up to the ones that scare you the most.

So the list could go like this:
Asking someone for the time
Asking someone for directions
Asking someone a question
Starting a conversation with a stranger
Asking a coworker how their weekend was
Singing Karaoke
Dancing in public
Speaking to the person I have a crush on at work
Giving a work presentation
Applying for a new job
Public speaking to strangers

Starting a conversation with a person I find attractive in a bar

# Step 2 — Rate Them on a Scale from 0 - 10

Once you've written the list, go through and number them from 0 to 10, with 10 being the most anxiety inducing and 0 the least. So it could go like this.

Asking someone for the time - 2
Asking someone for directions - 2.5
Asking someone a question - 3
Starting a conversation with a stranger - 4
Asking a coworker how their weekend was - 5
Singing Karaoke - 6
Dancing in public - 6.5
Speaking to the person I have a crush on at work - 7.5
Giving a work presentation - 8
Applying for a new job - 8.5
Public speaking to strangers - 9.5
Starting a conversation with a person I find attractive in a bar - 10

# Step 3 — Start with One Per Week or Fortnight

Start off with the smallest one first and do it at least three or four times during that week. If you need more time to feel comfortable, do it five or six times over a two-week period.

# Step 4 — Keep a Journal

Make a list of the event and the date. Describe your anxiety level out of 10 at three points. Beforehand, during, and after. Do the same the next three times you do it and compare the four results. You should see a reduction in your anxiety levels after the second, third, and fourth time you do it that week. If you haven't noticed a reduction, continue to do it for another week or so until you notice a reduction in anxiety.

## Step 5 — Move On to the Next

Once you feel you have that situation handled, move on to the next one on the list.

Repeat until you've ticked off all the things on the list. You don't have to do it all tomorrow; ease into it. One per week or one per fortnight is a good strategy. The exposures need to be just out of your comfort zone; however, it's better to be too much rather than too little. If it's not out of your comfort zone at all, it won't have much of an effect.

Try to find a supportive friend to hold you accountable so you'll actually follow through with it. Giving someone $100 to hold and if you don't do all the tasks they get to keep it is a good way to hold yourself accountable. Once you've ticked off the full list, add more challenging things to the list.

## More Advanced Things You Could Try

Join a public speaking program like Toastmasters
Join a gym or yoga class and do a workout
Apply for jobs
Go to a party or ball
Join a dancing class like salsa
Join a book club
Volunteer for a charity
Join a team sport
Take a cooking class
Get a part-time job in a bar
Join a flashmob
Take improv classes
Take a dating bootcamp
Join a debate team

## Tip: Hang in There

When doing these exercises, you need to stick it out for a solid amount of time. Singing karaoke for five seconds doesn't count as a complete task. You need to hang in there long enough to notice a reduction in your anxiety levels. This is where the real growth happens. Sometimes, this will mean a total of twenty minutes to two hours or more. The longer you can stay in a situation that causes you anxiety, the more confidence you'll gain. What you'll find is your anxiety will peak at a certain point, but as long as you hang in there, eventually your anxiety will massively decrease and you'll start to feel comfortable. Just like the horse we talked about in the fear section, you are rewiring your brain to no longer link social situations with fear.

For twenty-seven years, I never figured this out because I would always run away whenever I felt anxious. The first time I ever got past the peak of anxiety and felt comfortable in a social setting was one of the best experiences of my life. It was the first time I had ever been at a party where I didn't feel anxious. It helped me see I could be comfortable in social situations as long as I just stayed in there long enough and didn't give in to my anxiety.

When I did my first social exposure plan I had to do it alone. Nobody was there to support me or offer encouragement and I felt as if no-one cared if I succeeded or failed. The second one I did I had the support of a community and it was a thousand times easier to follow through. That's the reason I created the social anxiety academy. I did it for anyone wanting to go through the process of overcoming social anxiety with the support of a community who actually care about your success.

## *It Has to Be a Regular Thing*

You have to commit to doing these things on a regular basis, not once a year. Being sociable with new people has to be a regular thing.

Remember what I said about social skills? They're like a muscle, the more you use them, the stronger they get. If you don't use them, they become weak again.

I'm still committed to this; it's become part of my life now. I must keep being sociable because I don't want to slip back into my old avoidance patterns. I can't state this point enough:

*For every ounce of courage you can muster, you'll be rewarded in equal amounts with confidence and self-esteem. This is how we become socially confident.*

There's no better feeling I've ever experienced than the feeling of self-esteem you get from going after what you want in life, even when you're a little scared. I keep going on and on about growing self-esteem in this book because I believe it was so important in my healing.

# *Take It in Baby Steps & Celebrate the Small Victories*

*"80 percent of success is just showing up."* —Woody Allen

Celebrate every little victory. If I showed up to the club, that was a victory. If you haven't been out in a while, just leaving the house is a victory. Don't set the bar too high for yourself; just a little out of your normal comfort zone is okay. Just showing up to a dancing class and dancing with one person is a victory if you've never done that before. Remember to continue to keep raising the bar as you grow more confident so that it's always just out of your comfort zone. If you do, before you know it, you'll be doing stand-up comedy as I did. I know what you're thinking because I was thinking the same:

*"There's NO WAY on God's green earth I will ever do stand-up comedy in my life."*

But who knows? You may just surprise yourself with what you're capable of. Be proud of yourself and your small wins and build up from there.

# I Let Go of the Outcome

An important point to remember is this; growing your social confidence should never be judged on how well you did or how many people you impressed. If you muster the courage to ask someone out on a date, don't make it about the outcome because that's something you can't control. Just be happy that you went for it. Pat yourself on the back and say:

*"I'm proud of you!"*

How many times have you said that to yourself in your life? For me, it was close to zero. In fact, I would have thought it was cheesy to say that to myself. Now I say, "I'm proud of you," after every single thing I do that intimidates me. Every time you show courage, you deserve to be rewarded and praised for your effort, regardless of the outcome. Why? Because showing courage is not an easy thing to do and if it goes unnoticed and unpraised, what's your incentive to keep doing it?

Remember, let go of the outcome and make this process about the only thing you can control, YOU. If the only way you can feel happy or proud of yourself is by getting the result you're after, then you're setting yourself up for failure right off the bat. You can't control other people and whether or not they like you. The real successful outcome is that you went for it, even though you felt a little scared!

# You Win Some, You Lose Some—Either Way, People Don't Care

As I got out into the world and talked to lots of people, I realized I had been having double standards with myself all my life. I wasn't out there constantly judging everyone, but I thought everyone was constantly judging me.

I discovered over time, most people are just the same as me. Other people aren't analyzing every word I say and every step I take. They're not overly concerned with me and my flaws; they have their own problems and flaws to worry about. People have awkward conversations every day; life goes on and by tomorrow, it's all forgotten about anyway. You're the only one who remembers those times you were awkward.

# We Learn by Doing

Don't believe what anyone tells you. You cannot spend your life sitting at home in front of your book/TV/computer and expect to be magically healed. If you truly want to be free from your shyness and anxiety, this is going to take some action on your part. Don't get me wrong, reading and educating yourself is important, but it's only a part of it.

I thought I had to read every book ever written on social anxiety before I could act, but it was this kind of perfectionist thinking that got me stuck in the first place. There will always be another book we think we need to read, but books don't change our lives by themselves. We only grow from experience and by doing, from putting what we've learned into action.

After reading this book and working out an action plan of manageable goals for yourself, I recommend the 50/50 rule as previously mentioned. Spend 50 percent of your free time taking action (no matter how small) and 50 percent reading and looking inward. You know the kind of life that is waiting for you if you don't change or do anything differently—the exact life you have now.

## Keep Seeing the Big Picture—It's a Gradual Process, Not an On-Off Switch

Don't be disheartened if you go to bed feeling great about yourself one night, then you're not feeling so great about yourself the next. This is normal; we're overcoming decades of bad thought patterns and beliefs. Growing your confidence and self-esteem and getting rid of bad thought patterns that no longer serve you isn't an on-off process. You'll find that, over time, and as long as you do the work, you'll go from feeling confident only, say, 10 percent of the time to 30 percent, then you'll be feeling confident 50 percent of the time, and, eventually, 70-80-90 percent of the time.

You should never expect to feel confident 100 percent of the time because life just doesn't work like that. There will always be bad days, but the key is lifelong learning and continuing to work on yourself every day. So in summary, social confidence is a gradual process, like turning up the volume on a stereo rather than an on-off light switch.

## Summary

At the end of the day, you can read all the books you want, you can take all the programs you can find, but YOU have to find a way to spark the fire within you to take action towards your dreams. No one else can fix you and no one else can do it for you. Only you have the power to do that. It's not enough to just read this book and nod your head. You need to take what I'm showing you and put it to work in your life to make a positive change.

I understand there's a lot of information in this book and you may be feeling overwhelmed. You don't have to do all of this at once. Take it in baby steps. Just take on what you can handle for now.

*If you need any help with anything we've discussed so far, head over to* members.socialanxietyacademy.com, *create a free account and post a message on the community chat to ask me any questions.*

*3*

# HEALTHY DIET

## *Lifestyle & Diet Play a Huge Part*

I DON'T THINK MANY PEOPLE place as much importance as they should on the effect lifestyle and diet choices have on anxiety. A healthy diet, regular exercise, nature, sunlight, and living a balanced life were huge factors that reduced my generalized anxiety and depression symptoms.

## *Antidepressants*

I think the first thing we need to talk about is medication. I'm not a psychiatrist, so all I can give you is my opinion as a consumer, as someone who was on and off them for many years. First, before trying anything, you should always do your own research and not take anyone else's word for it.

Here are some issues I had with using antidepressant medication:

- My body built a tolerance to them, so I had to continually increase the dosage. In the end I was taking 5x the dose I started on.
- Coming off medication caused me severe withdrawal symptoms and dizziness.

147

- They were not good for my health and came with other side effects like loss of sex drive.
- A yearly supply of medication ended up being expensive.
- They made me feel flat and numb.

Many people say antidepressant medication helps to reduce their social anxiety symptoms, and that's great. Honestly, if it makes you feel better, gives you relief from anxiety, and allows you to feel more comfortable in social situations, then it's a good thing. Personally, I would recommend looking at your lifestyle and diet choices first, before reaching for the pills. I believe medication should be used as a last resort when nothing else works.

If you're currently on medications and would one day like to get off them, don't stop taking them right now. Instead, see if there's anything you can change in your life and diet that may be contributing to your anxiety. Hopefully, soon you may be able to reduce the dosage and, eventually, be free of them.

## Xanax

The benzo family of drugs really helped calm me down if I was having a panic attack or an anxiety attack. For times of intense anxiety, they work really well. But please remember, they're very addictive and I felt like a zombie afterward. Many people have serious addictions to these, so be warned.

## Natural Antidepressants

Here is a list of some natural alternatives to pharmaceutical antidepressants that have been said to work without all the side effects. These are definitely worth considering; however, do not take these if you're already on pharmaceutical antidepressants without consulting your doctor first.

**Inositol aka vitamin B8** - A natural antidepressant. Research has shown that people who suffer from anxiety, depression, and OCD symptoms have low levels of inositol in their body. Well worth looking into further.

**5-HTP** - A natural antidepressant. Getting positive reviews without the side effects of SSRIs (selective serotonin reuptake inhibitors).

**SAMe** - Another natural antidepressant said to be good for OCD conditions.

**GABA** - A natural relaxant for overstimulated people.

**Underactive Thyroid** - Another factor worth considering is the relationship an underactive thyroid has with anxiety and depression. People with underactive or overactive thyroids have been shown to have higher amounts of anxiety and depression than those with normally functioning thyroids. I would advise taking a test to see if your thyroid is functioning normally.

## Further reading

A book I highly recommend that covers all of this and more is *The Mood Cure* by Julia Ross M.A. I got a lot of great info about diet and natural mood lifters in this book.

# *Alcohol*

Drinking large amounts of alcohol tends to make people feel depressed the next day and worsens their anxiety symptoms. For many people, getting drunk is a massive crutch. They need it before they can feel confident, before they can dance, be themselves, and talk to strangers. I'm living proof you actually don't need alcohol. I've been out many times, danced, talked to strangers, and felt totally comfortable at parties and in nightclubs without even a sip of alcohol. This is coming from someone who had severe social anxiety just a few years ago. Go out and try it for yourself, you may be surprised.

But first rid yourself of the labels "I could never do that" or "I need alcohol to have fun." It's simply not true. Just have a few drinks; you don't have to get wasted to have fun. In my experience, "just having a few" is a very slippery slope, so set a limit for yourself of two or three drinks spread out over the whole night. You'll also be able to spend the money you saved by not drinking on something more worthwhile, like saving for a trip overseas.

## *Recreational Drugs*

You shouldn't be doing recreational drugs if you have anxiety or depression, especially if you're on any antidepressant medication.

**Marijuana** - Strong marijuana contributed to my obsessional thoughts and panic attacks.

**Caffeine** - Makes my general anxiety and obsessional thoughts worse, so I cut that out.

I can't emphasize this point enough; don't do recreational drugs if you have anxiety. It will only make it far, far worse in the long run. Like I said, we can overcome genetics as long as we stay healthy—both mentally and psychically.

# *Healthy Eating*

Healthy eating is a massively underrated way to reduce general anxiety. It's not given anywhere near the attention it deserves. Changing my diet played a big part in lowering my general anxiety disorder. I now consume a natural-food-based diet consisting of fresh fruit and vegetables with the rare fish meal, but no red meat or processed foods. Other people are also saying it has lowered their general anxiety levels.

I also do regular detoxification of my liver and colon. I feel much healthier, plus, since I cut out all these processed foods and sugar, I've lost a lot of body fat. Also, remember to drink plenty of water, two to four liters per day has been said to lower anxiety too.

Before judging or taking someone else's word for it, why don't you try it for yourself for a few weeks and see if it lowers your symptoms. What have you got to lose?

## Foods to Avoid
*All processed foods*
*Stimulants such as coffee*
*Refined white sugar and soft drinks*
*Alcohol & other drugs*
*Red meat*

## Further Reading
If you want more info on this topic, read *The Plant-Based Journey: A Step-By-Step Guide for Transitioning to a Healthy Lifestyle and Achieving Your Ideal Weight*.

I also recommend reading *Bugs, Bowels, and Behavior: The Groundbreaking Story of the Gut-Brain Connection*. This book states there's a link between your stomach and your brain. Apparently, an unhealthy stomach without enough good bacteria can affect your mood as most of our serotonin is found in our gut.

# 4

# LIFESTYLE CHOICES

I<small>T'S COMMON FOR PEOPLE</small> with social anxiety to also have another form of anxiety along with it. It was true for me. Here are some of the lifestyle choices I made that reduced all forms of my anxiety and depression. These aren't big things; everyone has time for them. If you think you don't have time, you need to figure out a way to make time, as they're really important for your overall health too.

## *I Cut Out Stress from My Life*

Stress has become so commonplace in our society and our workplaces that it's accepted as normal. Everyone seems to be "stressed out" and "busy" now days. Because stress is so accepted, people assume it can't be that bad for you. Stress is one of those things that's okay until it's not. Everything is under control until you get some kind of stress-related illness. Or maybe you already have an anxiety condition and you don't realize stress is making it even worse. Or stress might be the reason it's there in the first place.

The Congressional Prevention Coalition estimated that 90 percent of disease is caused or complicated by stress.[8] Research by Perkins showed that 60 to 90 percent of doctor visits were stress related.[9] Rosch found job stress to be far and away the leading source of stress for adults.[10]

Stress takes many forms. It can be disguised as frustration, anger, irritability, overwhelm, or always being in a hurry. All of these could be contributing to your anxiety. If you're currently working a stressful job, you need to ask yourself what it's costing you to get paid? *Are you getting paid, or are you the one who's actually paying with your health?*

Keep in mind there are ways to work in a stressful environment without allowing yourself to be run down by stress. Practices like meditation work wonders for stress relief. If you're allowing stress to get the better of you, there have been whole books written on the subject of stress management, and I recommend looking into them.

## Further Reading

*The Relaxation and Stress Reduction Workbook* by Martha Davis, Elizabeth Robbins Eshelman and Matthew McKay

# I Turned off the News and Stopped Reading Internet Comments

As a society, we are becoming more and more disconnected from nature and from each other. The 6 o'clock news is a one-hour report of the most horrific things that happened in the world that day. The news focuses on the worst parts of humanity and ignores the best. Every time we turn on the news, we're greeted by a new threat of a terror attack, videos of bombing the Middle East or elsewhere, schoolyard shootings, murders, and rapes.

If you're already fearful and have a predisposition to be anxious, don't stir it up by feeding your mind all the negativity and fear that the news offers you on an hourly basis. Do you really need to know who got murdered and raped that day or what school was shot up this week? Filling our minds with this negativity makes us constantly fearful and

154

distrusting of everyone. We become fearful of being raped, shot, robbed or stabbed every time we walk on the streets. Turn the news off, and you'll feel much better for it.

Some people tell me, "I have to stay informed." Trust me, as someone who never watches the news, you'll be told of the things you really need to be informed about. What I would ask is; what's more important to you, overcoming anxiety or watching the news?

## #neverreadthecomments

Furthermore, stop reading the comments on blog posts and such. Most of it is negative venting written by trolls who would never actually say that stuff in real life. Don't fill your mind with that negativity. People have committed suicide over what people write to them online. Facebook bullying has become epidemic in schools. If you're already concerned with people judging you in day-to-day life, don't read Internet comments. The number of negative comments way outweighs the positive ones, and it can give you the wrong idea about people and how much they judge. That's not how it is in real life.

Just don't go there anymore and you'll be better off for it.

## *Exercise — I Went to the Gym*

Thirty minutes to one hour of exercise three to five times per week plays a huge role in controlling anxiety levels. Strenuous exercise like running has been proven to increase serotonin and endorphins (the feel-good chemicals in your brain). Exercise makes you feel great and actually increases your energy. When you feel good, you're more willing to go out and socialize. No one wants to socialize when they feel depressed and lethargic.

Going to the gym was HUGE for me. This changed my whole life. I never considered myself attractive before, so I decided to do something about it and made a commitment to go to the gym four times a week. After only a couple of months, I saw real results. My muscles became bigger and more toned, the fat fell off, and things firmed up. The results were twofold. I became proud of how I was looking in the mirror plus I felt great and mentally sharp after a workout. This made me want to go even more, as I was seeing and feeling the benefits.

I can't recommend this enough for both men and women. If you're new to fitness and working out and would like to find out more about it, I recommend checking out www.bodybuilding.com. Don't be put off by the name, it's not just about bodybuilding. It's an amazing website on how to get fit and healthy. There you'll find loads of free programs and workouts you can do for both men and women. They give you everything you need to know to get started on your fitness journey, including the correct exercises and diet advice.

# 30 Minutes of Sunlight and Nature Every Day

I think this is a really important one. It has been proven that some people suffer from what's called seasonal depression. During winter, when there's little sun and it's cold, people get depressed and their anxiety worsens. Sunlight has been proven to raise serotonin levels (the happy chemical in our brains). Spending at least thirty minutes outdoors in the sunlight 3 to 5 times a week has been very helpful for me and my mood.

I choose to run outside instead of indoors on the treadmill. I go and watch sunsets at the beach. I get out into nature and go hiking and climb mountains. I go and sit in the park and have a cup of tea.

There was great healing for me here. If you don't have sun where you live or it's winter, you can buy UV lights that do almost the same thing for your body as sunlight. Try to spend less time on the computer indoors and get out into nature. We weren't meant to be cooped up inside all day every day.

# I Decided to Work Fewer Hours

*"No one on their deathbed ever wished they spent more time at the office."* —Wayne Dyer

I used to think money would make all my problems go away. So I became a chronic over-worker, working ten to fourteen hours per day. For years, I worked two jobs. I would wake up in the morning and begin working right away until I would have to sleep again that night, only stopping for meals. Anytime I decided to take a day off work for some fun, I would feel guilty about it and feel like I was being lazy. Work and making money became all consuming.

This chronic overworking was severely affecting my mental health. Not only was it affecting my health, I also realized I was using work as an excuse so I didn't have to socialize. I rearranged my priorities and my life and chose a career where I could have more free time. Productivity has been shown to decrease dramatically after working the first eight hours of your day and health risks increase with each additional hour worked per day, especially if you're sitting while working. If working less isn't an option for you, consider putting less stress on yourself while you're at work and focus on the quality of your hours, not the quantity. Our health is the most valuable thing we have.

Also remember to make sure you get at least eight hours of sleep every night. There have been studies done on the link between anxiety, depression and lack of sleep. Remember, not all sleep is equal; you need deep sleep. I would recommend investing in a good set of earplugs and an eye mask to block out any light and background noise. This will make it easier for you to get that deep, regenerative sleep that your body needs every night to repair and heal itself.

# I Began Meditating Every Day

Meditation is simply quieting your mind for a few minutes. It has a new age stigma around it, but monks and hippies aren't the only ones who meditate. Fortune 500 CEOs use it, top athletes use it, stay-at-home moms use it. Hugh Jackman, Jim Carrey, Goldie Hawn, Russell Brand, and Tony Robbins (just to name a few) are all massive advocates of daily meditation.

Meditation is so important for everyone, especially those with mental health issues. My thoughts used to just run nonstop for days (and they still do). Sometimes, I couldn't even sleep because my mind would be racing, mostly with negative thoughts about myself or what someone said or did to me. Meditation helps me quiet my busy mind for some much-needed relief from the constant barrage of thoughts. When you completely quiet your mind and stop your thoughts, even just for a few seconds, everything feels much lighter.

Meditation has allowed me to become more centered, and stress doesn't affect me as much. I can handle whatever I encounter in my day and I worry less about what everyone else is thinking of me. Meditation makes it easier to let go of things because you're training your mind to stop thinking. I really recommend that you try meditation; it could just change your life.

Currently, I meditate for twenty to thirty minutes per day. To someone who's never done that before, it might seem like a long time to be sitting there doing nothing. You also might be thinking you don't have that sort of spare time to waste. But I guarantee you'll be so much more effective in your life once you start meditating that you won't know how you lived without it. You'll get more done in less time and feel much better doing it.

# Benefits of Meditation

### Presence
We're in the ADD generation. There's so much information at our fingertips that it's easy to become overwhelmed. Most of us can't sit through a thirty-minute meal without checking our phones several times. Meditation helps you get centered and stay present. Learning to be present is essential for not getting swept up in anxious thoughts and being a good communicator.

### Meditation Keeps You Emotionally Calm
I don't really get angry at little annoyances in life anymore. If a situation annoys me, I have the ability to just let the feeling go and carry on. A simple technique in a stressful situation is to take a deep breath in, hold for four seconds, take a long breath out, then repeat one more time.

### Productivity Can Benefit from Mediation
We're always so busy these days with so much to do and so little time. It's tough to be on seven days a week. What helps me when I lose focus is a ten-minute meditation. This clears my mind, calms my thoughts, allows me to re-focus and keeps me from being overwhelmed with all the things I need to get done.

### A Shower for Your Mind
We must bathe our bodies daily, so why should it be anything different with our minds? As we go about our day, we collect all kinds of junk

and muck in our minds. A negative comment from someone, stress from our busy lives and poor self-talk. These things need to be cleaned out daily by "resetting" and getting back to our breathing. Your mind runs and runs all day nonstop. Meditation is like turning your engine off for a few minutes for a rest and oil change.

## Developing the Habit

It's hard to stop your thoughts, even for ten seconds. If you're a chronic over-thinker and someone whose mind races, sitting down for twenty minutes and trying not to think is really hard in the beginning. Like everything I've discussed in the book, we need to start off small and then improve a little bit each day. After a few months, you'll get to a point where it will be the thing you look forward to most in your day. It will feel like taking a nice warm bath for your mind; it's total bliss.

## How I Do It

1. I find a quiet place. I simply sit cross-legged with my back straight on my lounge or bed. Sometimes, I'll light a candle if it's night. I relax my whole body, my eyes, my face, my shoulders, etc. I relax as much as I can.
2. I put my phone and computer on silent to not be disturbed.
3. I set the countdown timer for the number of minutes I want to go for.
4. Hit the start button and close my eyes.
5. All I focus on is my breath – "breathing iiiiinnnnn – breathing ouuutttt." Try not to focus or think about anything other than your breath.
6. Your mind WILL wander. That's normal; don't judge yourself or feel bad about it. Once you catch your mind thinking about something else, allow yourself to come back to focusing on your breath again. Remember, no judgment!

In the beginning, I got bored easily and found it very hard to stay focused. I gave up a few times before the habit stuck. I was trying to run before I could walk by trying to do twenty minutes right away when I should have started with five minutes and gone from there.

Here's the best way to learn meditation:

Day 1 – 7: 5 minutes
Day 8 – 14: 7 minutes
Day 15 – 30: 10 minutes
Day 30 +: 15 - 20 minutes

For this to be effective, it has to be a daily thing. Figure a way to fit it into your routine. It could be when you first wake up, the last thing before you sleep, or during your lunch break. For best results, try all three times. When I meditate before I sleep, it helps me fall asleep quicker. When I meditate after lunch, I don't get as lethargic. And meditating in the morning puts me in a good mood and sets me up for a good day.

If you miss a day or two, it's okay, no judgment. Just get back on it as soon as you can. When you feel like skipping a day, just think about all the rewards that come with meditation: less stress, less anxiety, increased focus, and just generally feeling better.

## *Living a Balanced Life*

I spent some of my time with friends, some of my time meeting new people. I spent some time exercising, some time alone reading, and some time working. All our great healers tell us how important it is to have a balanced life. I tried to do everything I could to feel good. I took long baths, listened to my favorite music as much as I could, got massages, and treated myself to nice things. And I still do all of these things today.

Most importantly, I accepted myself for exactly who I am and stopped judging myself and calling myself harsh names.

# IN CLOSING

I WANT TO THANK YOU for showing the courage to seek help because it's not always an easy thing to do. See, you do have courage! I want you to know, no matter how bad things seem right now, there is a light at the end of the social anxiety tunnel. I know because I was once deep in the tunnel with no light to be seen and I found my way out. I hope I've given you some inspiration by sharing my story and what worked for me.

It may seem like there's a lot of information in this book and not all of it may resonate with you right now. Try to keep an open mind and don't be too quick to judge things you've never tried before; you just might end up benefitting from them. Remember, you don't have to do it all at once. Take a few things that stick out to you and work on those first. And, when you're ready, take on some more.

I've given you a roadmap to follow but you must take the journey yourself; no one else can fix you or do it for you. All I can tell you is that *it will happen* as long as you don't give up, and when it does, it will be GLORIOUS. Even more beautiful will be the journey there and seeing yourself turn into the person you've always wanted to be right before your eyes. The good times wouldn't feel so sweet without the bad times; and boy, is it going to feel sweet when you get this handled.

## One Thought I'd Like to Leave You With...
*Happiness, joy, love, and well-being is our birthright; it's never something we have to earn or become worthy of.*

You're unique and special, there's only one of you in the whole world. Celebrate that fact! I know that sounds a little cliche but it's true. Share your light with the world; be exactly who you are and who you were born to be. Share the gifts that are unique to only you, and the world will be a better place because of you. Perhaps one day soon we will be working side-by-side, spreading our message that healing is possible, and empowering people to remember their true value and worth.

I truly hope this book helps you find your healing. If I can do it, you can too.

Love yourself always.

Tobias

P.S - I've put my heart and soul into this book. If you feel it has helped you, please pay it forward by passing this information on to anyone who may need it, or by leaving a book review so others going through similar conditions can also benefit. Knowing I made a positive difference in someone's life will make the months I spent writing this all worthwhile.

## *Further Guidance*

If you need any further guidance, someone to help you along your journey, or just want to make some new friends. I personally invite you to join our community of encouraging and supportive people at the Social Anxiety Academy.

I will be there to give you support and encouragement. I look forward to meeting you and hearing your success story. Visit www.socialanxietyacademy.com for more details.

# END NOTES

1. Anxiety and Depression Association of America. (2014, September). Facts & statistics. Retrieved from http://www.adaa.org/about-adaa/press-room/facts-statistics

2. Mayo Clinic Staff. (2014, September). Social anxiety disorder (social phobia). Retrieved from http://www.mayoclinic.org/diseases-conditions/social-anxiety-disorder/basics/definition/con-20032524

3. Sugar, R., Feloni, R., & Lutz, A. (2015, July 9). 29 famous people who failed before they succeeded. Retrieved from http://www.businessinsider.com/successful-people-who-failed-at-first-2015-7

4. Fortson, L. (2012, February 7). Epigenetics. Retrieved from https://www.brucelipton.com/resource/article/epigenetics

5. Dyer, W. (1994) *Pulling your own strings*. New York, NY: Harper Collins.

6. *Psychology Today* (n.d.) Perfectionism. Retrieved from https://www.psychologytoday.com/basics/perfectionism

7. Maltz, M. (2002). *The new psycho-cybernetics*. New York, NY: Prentice Hall.

8. Congressional Prevention Coalition. (1998). Stress prevention. Retrieved from http://istpp.org/coalition/stress_prevention.html

9. Perkins, A. (1994) Saving money by reducing stress. *Harvard Business Review, 72*(6), 12.

10. Rosch, P. J. (1991, May). Job stress: America's leading adult health problem, *USA Magazine.*

17331292R00100

Printed in Great Britain
by Amazon